HOW TO ENJOY PEACE IN YOUR LIFE EVERY DAY

George E. Wallace

Copyright ©2005 George E. Wallace

All rights reserved. No part of this book may be reproduced or transmitted in any form or by any means, electronic or mechanical, including photocopying, recording, or by any information storage and retrieval system, without permission in writing from the publisher.

ISBN# 0-9770937-0-0

Cover Design: Lynn Walters
Cover Photograph: Elaine Wallace
Text Layout: Nicole Deveau
Production Assistant: Rachael Boisvert

Park Avenue
Publishing, Inc.

100 Main Street
Reading, MA 01867

Printed in Canada

*For Elaine.
You taught me how to love.
This book would not have been
possible without you.*

ACKNOWLEDGMENTS

I could not have written this book without the understanding and support of my wife and children. Although my wife, Elaine, has been too scared to actually read the book, her encouragement has been invaluable. My daughters, Sabrina and Rebecca, would much rather have me shooting hoops with them in the driveway. But they have been remarkably good about not interrupting me while I am working.

My editor, Lloyd Resnick, has been a godsend. This is my first book and I was really nervous about having someone actually edit my work. But I am truly amazed at the difference Lloyd has made in a very quiet and unassuming manner. I never would have believed that an editor could weave such magic.

I also need to thank Jim Degnan, Kathy Messana, and Pat Conway for reading the manuscript and providing running commentary. Rose Cravens really poured her heart into showing me some changes I needed to make. Lynn Walters brought her usual creative magic to the design of the cover and the brochure I produced to help market the book. Elaine Wallace found a way to make me look somewhat presentable through the lens of her camera and the voodoo of *Photoshop*. Nicole Deveau did a remarkable job producing the electronic layout while working under a rather tight deadline. And Rachael Boisvert has been very helpful in many of the details.

TABLE OF CONTENTS

INTRODUCTION — 11

CHAPTER ONE

CHOOSE PEACE — 17

- OOOPS! — 21
- BEEN THERE, DONE THAT — 27
- THE CHARACTERISTICS OF A LIFE BASED ON PEACE — 33
- THE GOOD NEWS AND THE BAD NEWS — 37
- CHOOSING PEACE CONNECTS YOU TO YOUR REAL SELF — 43
- ONE MAN'S DECISION IS STRONGER THAN AN ARMY — 47
- MY CHOICE FOR PEACE — 53
- YOU WILL KNOW PEACE AND SERENITY — 59

CHAPTER TWO

MAKE A COMMITMENT TO YOUR CHOICE — 63

- THE MEMORABLE DATE — 67
- PUTTING DOWN THE DRINK — 73
- MEET THE TAG TEAM — 77
- LIFE AS A DRY DRUNK: IT ISN'T FUN — 83
- THE LESSON OF THE STORIES, THE STORY OF THE LESSONS — 91
- ONE OF MANY MIRACLES — 95
- DECIDING HOW TO THINK — 99
- HOW I MET MY WIFE: ANOTHER MIRACLE — 105
- YOU JUST NEVER KNOW — 111
- THE COMMITMENT — 117

CHAPTER THREE

THE ILLUSION OF CONTROL — 131

- THE PLAN — 135
- THE VOICE OF THE EGO — 149
- THE PRE-EMPTIVE STRIKE — 153

continued...

CHAPTER THREE

THE ILLUSION OF CONTROL   *continued...*

THE UNCOVERED TOOTHPASTE	159
THE REAL DEAL	163
CONTROL IS AN ILLUSION	165
THE MACROCOSM AND THE MICROCOSM ARE THE SAME	171
EXAMPLES OF REAL-LIFE DECISIONS FOR PEACE	179
YOU ARE NOT YOUR EGO	187
THAT WHICH YOU CAN CONTROL	195

CHAPTER FOUR

THE OUTSIDE REFLECTS THE INSIDE   **203**

THE BABY KILLER	207
MAKING THE CHANGE PERMANENT	213
I THINK I AM GOING TO LIVE	217
NOPE, LOOKS LIKE I AM GOING TO DIE	229
GOD WAS THERE ALL ALONG	231
ITS ABOUT TIME!	235
AN INCREDIBLE STRING OF "COINCIDENCES"	239
MEETING MY SPONSOR	241
THE END OF THE BEGINNING	245
THE WORLD IS YOUR MIRROR	251
THE ROLE OF FORGIVENESS	257

CHAPTER FIVE

PEACE IS THE WAY   **261**

I NEVER SAW IT COMING	265
THIS IS MUCH BIGGER THAN ME	271
THE POSITION OF PEACE IS THE POSITION OF STRENGTH	277
THE JUSTIFICATION FOR WAR	283
WHAT IF	291

INTRODUCTION

Life does not have to be so difficult.

You can be free.

Imagine looking at everything that occurs in your life and seeing only opportunity, possibility, and that which is positive and life-enhancing. Imagine being able to live from one day to the next without ever focusing on fear, anger, resentment, hatred, sadness, frustration, anxiety, or desperation as the characteristics that demand your attention. Imagine looking back on the day's activities and measuring all that occurred in terms of how good it was or how much you learned, rather than in degrees of crisis. And imagine how much more effective you can be in everything you do if you know, with every fiber of your being, that there isn't anything anyone can do or say that will adversely affect you in any way without your permission.

Gone are those instances where other people are able to push your buttons. Gone is the fear of financial insecurity and your attachment to results and self-limiting goals. Gone are the gut-wrenching feelings of loneliness, isolation, and desperation. Gone is the demanding and exhausting need to be in control.

You can *decide* to have emotional and spiritual freedom. Then you can make a commitment to your decision and sit back and watch as those freedoms are handed to you by a loving Force that is only too happy to see you thrive. You can experience excitement instead of trepidation, anticipate with hope rather than fear, and allow the love with which you were created to become the unshakable foundation of your life.

By changing the way you think, you will change your

perception of, and reaction to, the world around you. Happiness, peace, serenity, joy, compassion, and love will be your ever-present companions. And you can feel the exhilarating freedom of living with purpose rather than constantly allowing your reactions to what other people do or say dictate your thoughts and feelings. You can become the author and architect of your own emotional state, no matter what manner of chaos, dysfunction, or pure stupidity happens to be dropped in your lap.

Everyone enters this world pre-wired into their hearts and souls all of the love, peace, joy, happiness, serenity, and compassion that could ever be desired. Unfortunately, we spend a lifetime acquiring thought patterns and behaviors that do nothing but distance us from our Real Selves. We arrive as magnificent and totally loving souls and spirits. Then we spend the remainder of our time here shrinking the universe of available opportunity, severely diminishing our emotional range and capacity, and crowding ourselves into smaller and smaller spiritual places, without even knowing we are doing so.

An element of fear colors all our decisions, interactions, and relationships, and it has been with us for so long, we don't even notice its presence. Fear shows itself in our adverse reactions, negative thinking, and that nagging feeling that something is missing. Fear is only capable of shrinking and contracting. It is entirely incapable of engendering or supporting the expansion and extension for which we were originally created. Fear gets in the way.

Over the years, we learn to react to other people, places, and things in automatic ways. We spend most of our time watching out for ourselves, which in and of itself is an indication that fear is the prime motivator.

We do not know that our thinking, feelings, and emotions actually default to pre-determined settings, not unlike this laptop computer, which has a default font setting of *Times New Roman*. The only thing that really changes from one situation to the next is the intensity of the setting. We come to believe that such an existence is normal and do not expect it to be any different. We generally do not know there is another way - and we do not know that we do not know.

It often takes a book like this one, coming from an entirely different perspective, to show us that there is indeed another way, a way that was heretofore unavailable because we just didn't know it was there. You can actually *decide* what you think and how you feel on any given occasion. Living a life of peace is a byproduct of eliminating the default-type thinking that you are most likely unaware permeates your life. Living a life of peace means understanding, recognizing, and embracing your connection to your True Self. You can become the person God originally intended you to be - one day at a time, one thought at a time.

I began my life as a good kid. I was quiet, respectful, and decent. I enjoyed doing things for other people just for the sake of doing them. I had a highly upbeat and positive outlook, and I was considered rather bright and capable. Somewhere along the line I got my wires crossed and ended up spiraling into active alcoholism and a life of total misery. I ended up completely alone and suicidal. But God had other plans for me, and I am eternally grateful that I have been able to connect myself to His plan.

The Twelve Steps of Alcoholics Anonymous saved my life and provided a comprehensive guide that brought me back to the land of the living. But it wasn't enough. I needed more. Through a series of remarkable events

I began to study *A Course In Miracles*, which showed me how to change my thinking and forever banish the effects of fear in my life. My story is replete with coincidences that are not coincidences, spiritual epiphanies that are nothing short of incredible, and a growing conviction that the more I let go, the more I have. All I had to do was decide to live a life of peace, no matter what, and then get out of the way and allow it to flourish and take on a life of its own.

The stories I relate in this book are true. There are many lessons to be learned from the experiences and interpretations that fill these pages. The stories and lessons are for anyone and everyone. They are universal. They will help you lead a more meaningful life.

I was once reduced to abject emotional and spiritual bankruptcy. But I never gave up. I knew that the good little boy I had once been was alive and untouched somewhere inside. He was buried under a mountain of emotional rubble, but he was intact, alive, and he never stopped pushing to see the light of day. I am quite thankful today that the rubble is gone. Shame, embarrassment, fear, and regret have all gone away as well. I am free. And if I can do it, anybody can.

But having learned the things I have learned isn't enough, either. The idea of sharing in a book what has been so helpful in reclaiming my life came to me one day and would not go away. It lived inside and spoke to me all the time. I put it off as long as I could. I had triathlons to train for and businesses to run, a family to spend time with, and volunteer work to do. But the book kept speaking to me, and I finally went to it kicking and screaming. Eventually, I injured myself during a triathlon in Vermont, so I couldn't run. This "coincidence" provided me with the time to write - that is if you call getting up at 4:30 in the morning finding the time to write.

Writing this book has been a rather odd experience because, as the words came out of me and I typed them into my computer, I often found myself wondering where they could possibly have come from. They are not my words. They came *through* me rather than from me. The entire process has been a constant and total surprise. Whenever I sat down to write, I never really knew what was coming. It has been a very exciting and enjoyable experience.

A Course In Miracles teaches that if you want to learn something for yourself, teach it to someone else. If you want to learn love, teach love. If you want to learn peace, teach peace. I have learned much about love and peace by writing this book and providing you with my particular slant on how you can live a life that has heretofore seemed only an unattainable dream. I came from a place I wouldn't wish on anyone, and I have found myself in a place that I was totally incapable of imagining. Therefore, I believe I will eventually get to a place down the road that I cannot possibly fathom today. And all I have to do is exercise a little bit of willingness and keep following my nose. It is no more complicated than that for anyone.

I sincerely hope that the words in this book make a positive difference in your life. Writing them has helped me immensely.

I wish you well on your journey, and I thank you for helping me on my journey.

George Wallace

CHAPTER ONE

CHOOSE PEACE

Chapter One - Choose Peace

"The marvelous richness of human experience would lose something of rewarding joy if there were not limitations to overcome. The hilltop hour would not be half so wonderful if there were no dark valleys to traverse."

- Hellen Keller

"I can see peace instead of this."

- A Course In Miracles

"In the depths of winter I finally learned there was in me invincible summer."

- Albert Camus

"Faced with the choice between changing one's mind and proving there is no need to do so, almost everyone gets busy on the proof."

- John Kenneth Galbraith

Chapter One - Choose Peace

OOOPS!

Perhaps it was the pressure I felt on my forehead that woke me up. Very slowly, ever so gradually, I became more and more aware of it, like a stray fly that buzzes around your ear in the middle of the night and ends up annoying the living daylights out of you. Your first instinct is to make it go away, but you really don't want to completely wake up in order to facilitate its demise. You want to kill that nasty little fly, but waking up to do so is just too high a price to pay. I didn't feel any pain associated with the pressure; it was more bothersome than anything else. And it certainly didn't seem to be a source of any great concern to me - just a consistent gentle force exerted on the outer edges of my forehead. What the hell was it?

Reluctantly, my eyes began to pry themselves open in response to the increasingly palpable pressure. Although I really did not want to, I suppose I had to figure out what was going on and decide what to do about it. Perhaps it was only a dream. As my eyes began to slowly focus and my muddled vision began to clarify, I became increasingly aware of a superbly rich shade of blue. It dominated my entire field of vision from left to right, and from up to down. Were it not for the progressively uncomfortable pressure that I first noticed on the outer edges of my forehead, and which now seemed to have spread to the back of my neck, I would have found this shade of blue to be somewhat comfort evocative.

This was not just any ordinary blue, it was a deeply resonant royal blue, evoking images of pageantry, pomp, and circumstance throughout a human history dominated by the influences of the Hapsburg empire, the Windsors of merry old England, and the Romanov dynasty. But where was the blue coming from? And why was I so damn uncomfortable? And what were all those noises I could hear somewhere off in what seemed to be the very distant background? The rest of my senses began to revive and were it not for the pleasant color that would thankfully not go away, I can assure you that I was not a happy camper to be woken up under such unpleasant circumstances. Someone was going to pay, and pay big, for disturbing me like this.

But what was this blue thing? And what was that little puddle of red liquid that was slowly expanding in the middle of the pretty blue field, little by unstoppable little, seeking to transform such a handsome and noble color into an entirely uninteresting and boring brown blotch. And what could all those flashing blue and red lights be? And why was it so difficult to breathe?

Then it dawned on me. Nobody was shaking me or trying to interrupt my peaceful slumber in any way. I was sitting in the back seat of one of Boston's Finest's automobiles. It also occurred to me that I hadn't been invited to view the inside of a police car to either admire the view and marvel at all the little buttons and various gizmos that adorned such vehicles, or to take a little bit of a rest from an exhausting and backbreaking day. No, I began to understand that I wasn't sitting in the back seat of a police car with the radio bleating its unintelligible garble and blue lights pulsing signals of danger and authority into the cool evening air because Officer Friendly wanted to have a pleasant little chat.

Being a man of above average intelligence, it wasn't long before I was able to positively identify the source of the wonderful blue color and the slowly spreading puddle of red liquid that appeared in the middle of that pleasant blue field, both of which had held my interest for some time now. The blue thing

Chapter One - Choose Peace

was the carpet on the floor of the car that belonged to the City of Boston and the slowly spreading red was directly associated with the sensation of discomfort emanating from the region of my mouth.

It finally dawned on me that I was sitting in the back seat of a police car with my head resting on the backrest of the front seat, thereby explaining the pressure I was feeling on my forehead. I was staring down at the carpet on the floor and the mysterious red liquid was, not so surprisingly, blood. My blood. And it was steadily dripping from my tongue. I opened my mouth to speak but I was unable to do so because my jaw was entirely shattered.

So here I was, sitting in the back seat of an automobile registered to the City of Boston, sitting in an automobile with the unmistakable array of antennae and night-piercing, bright blue flashing lights, sitting with my head resting on the front seat and my arms resting on my knees in a car that had the authoritative and ominous words "Boston Police" clearly painted on every available piece of space, sitting there unable to raise my head off its resting place and not wanting to, sitting there having a very difficult time speaking the king's English because my jaw was smashed to smithereens, my tongue was severely cut, and I was still very, very drunk.

I sat there with at least a couple of broken ribs that I was able to count and an interesting variety of contusions and abrasions, knowing that I had just been involved in a very serious car accident and not having the foggiest notion as to how the accident happened. I sat there beside Cheryl, who had been my date that evening and who seemed to be doing somewhat better than I. I sat there wondering if I had bitten off part of my tongue and if they would ever be able to sew it back on. I wondered about the car I had been driving, my father's car, and contemplated the world of shit I was going to live in as a result of wrecking his car. And I sat there without a single clue as to exactly what had happened, and nobody seemed to be in a very big hurry to provide the information.

But wait! Could it have anything to do with the gallons of beer I had swilled down that night at the Beer Bust? A Beer Bust was the name given to a fund raising effort held by an organization of which I was a member. The idea was that we charge $10 a person, provide a DJ for the evening's entertainment, and the rivers of beer that flowed from the multitudinous kegs purchased for just this occasion didn't cost a penny more. What a deal! If I remember correctly, there was even some kind of food available as well, but nobody really cared much about that.

I was 19 years old, full of piss and vinegar, and I had an attitude of absolute indestructibility. Cheryl was a girl that I had just begun dating, and she was as beautiful a person on the inside as she was on the outside. I just couldn't believe she was going out with me when there were so many others, with obviously more to offer than I had, from which she could have her choice. Going to a Beer Bust on a Saturday night, partying and dancing with all my friends, and spending a wonderful evening with Cheryl Fraser - this was about as good as it could ever get. Yet there we were, sitting in the back seat of Officer Friendly's garishly painted mobile motor circus, and I was the animal caged inside.

Lying in the emergency room at the Carney Hospital in Dorchester, I apologized to my father about the car and told him that I think I had a little bit too much to drink. He told me not to worry about the car. He was glad that I hadn't been

Chapter One - Choose Peace

killed and told me that I was not to mention anything about the drinking thing to anyone, anytime, no matter what. Worked for me. I agreed and went on from there.

It took a special oral surgeon from another hospital and seven hours on the operating table to put Humpty Dumpty's jaw back together again. My jaw was wired shut, severely clamped down with heavy duty elastic bands, and the only nourishment that could pass through this formidable apparatus had to be entirely liquid. Beer is liquid. But I was terrified to drink any kind of alcoholic beverage, let alone get drunk, because if I were to get sick and have to puke my guts up, it would have nowhere to go because my jaw was wired shut and I might well end up drowning in my own spew.

I did not think such an experience would feel all that great. So I avoided drinking alcohol entirely until I came up with an idea even more brilliant than the electric light bulb. All I had to do was make sure I had a straight razor in my pocket. Then, if I decided to go drinking with my friends, which is one of the things we were really good at, and it should transpire that I was going to be sick to my stomach, I would whip that trusty old straight razor out of my pocket just as fast as Wyatt Earp drawing his six shooter to gun down the Clantons at the OK Corral, and I would simply slice through all those elastic bands clamping my jaws together. I would be free to be as sick as I wanted to be. What a great idea!

Well, I put the razor in my pocket every time I went drinking, but I never did get a chance to try out my foolproof plan of self preservation. It is probably just as well because the way I used to drink, I am sure that I would have succeeded in slicing off my nose rather than actually cutting through those elastic bands.

Like I said, I was 19 years old and indestructible. Unbeknownst to me at the time was the fact that I was also on the threshold of a 12 year alcoholic drinking career. A career that would feature more calamities with automobiles, a marriage that lasted only nine months before ending up in a nasty divorce, and a life so filled with near-death situations that to have survived is certainly miraculous.

But this is not a "true confessions" kind of soul-purging book. I have already gone through that process, and I feel no need to go through it again except inasmuch as my past adventures, both the good and the bad, will serve as appropriate and entertaining ways to make a particular point. Some of the stories I will relate are actually more than a little entertaining. Some are downright amazing. The point is that the shame and guilt I lived with for so many years is gone - entirely gone. The anger, fear, rage, confusion, frustration, and feelings of being "less than" that were the hallmark of my existence for such a long time are gone as well. And I can honestly tell you that the most predominant feeling that exists for me today, and every day, is that of peace.

Chapter One - Choose Peace

BEEN THERE, DONE THAT

One of the things we will firmly establish during the course of this book is that nobody is any better or any worse than anybody else. We are all very much brothers and sisters under the skin. Therefore, if I can make the transition I have made in my life, a transition that will be described in this book, anybody can. There is nothing special about me. I just happen to have been fortunate enough to figure some things out, and I am looking to share them with you because in doing so I get to learn them all over again.

It is my intention to show you exactly how I was able to make the transition from absolute lunatic to living a life of pure possibility and opportunity by using my actual experience as the instruction manual. I will put it all out there and hide nothing because there is nothing about which I feel the slightest bit of shame. As the pages unfold, I will also show you that your very own personal history proves to you that you surely can live a life based on an increased experience and understanding of peace, love, joy, compassion, and serenity. You will learn to look at your life from a different perspective, and everything will change for you. All you need to bring to the party is a little bit of willingness.

If someone is going to teach me something, I am the kind of guy that needs to know that he or she can actually do what they are teaching. I need to be shown. I need to see them in action, actively demonstrating the skill that they are trying to impart. I am really not much of a proponent of the phrase "them that can, do, and them that can't, teach." This is why I change the television channel just as fast as humanly possible when I happen to come across one of those TV evangelists preaching up a storm and asking for money. I always have the impression that they talk a good game, but when the cameras stop rolling and the pancake make-up comes off, they go home and kick the dog.

If someone is going to teach me some extraordinarily valuable lessons about how I can live my life more effectively; eliminate shame and guilt forever; make kindness, dignity, respect, and love the experiences that permeate the very fabric of my life every day; and help me wake up in the morning with a sense of excitement rather than foreboding, then I am going to want to know *how* that person came about acquiring such incredible knowledge. I am also going to want to be shown, in no uncertain terms, that this teacher actively lives that which he or she teaches. I very much need to know that they have been there, done that - that they walk the proverbial talk.

Through the pages of this book, I will show you exactly how I have been able to change my thinking and thereby change my life. In no way am I suggesting that my way is the only way. It is not. However, I do know that what I have done has worked for me in ways I never could have imagined, and a variation of it can work for you. It is my experience that long-term, fully integrated change that you can count on day in and day out is not possible unless you change the thinking that got you to the point of seeking a change in the first place. We need to change the software in order to change the default settings that have gotten us this far and don't seem to be working for us any more.

If you are still reading, you are looking for something. Many people have found that which you seek because it is not hiding. It is right there, already inside you, patiently waiting for you to come home. The only problem is that we have simply forgotten our true nature, which is love. Our only job is to

Chapter One - Choose Peace

remember that which has always lived inside, because it is who we really are. My hope is that I can help you remember your Real Self. I promise you that, one day at a time, one person at a time, one thought at a time, your life can transform into something about which you have previously only dreamed. You can live a life of peace, love, joy, happiness, and serenity - no matter what happens to be going on in the world at large or in your every day affairs. This I promise.

I once went to Stow Acres Country Club in Stow, Massachusetts to sign up for a weekend long golf clinic because I needed help in a huge way. I was looking for a golf lobotomy, anything that would help me to learn what was then an increasingly perplexing and seemingly unavailable skill. The school split the class up into smaller groups and assigned a club pro as the instructor for each group. Right from the get-go the pro assigned to my group, a man whose name currently escapes me, actively demonstrated his skill. He clearly showed all of us that he could drop a seven iron shot anywhere he wanted in relation to the pin. Like me and most of the rest of the world he was a right-handed golfer and when he said he would put his shot three feet to the right of the pin, then by golly he did just that. He was beginning to gain my interest.

We had one left-handed golfer in the group, and the pro patiently explained to him that the dynamic of his shot was slightly different because he was left-handed. So when the instructor took this guy's left-handed seven iron, turned the other way to make his shots as a lefty, and did so with as much dexterity and accuracy as he did as a right-handed golfer, I knew that I would listen to him and try my absolute best to do exactly what he told me to do. He had proven himself to me.

The reason I chose to begin this book with the story of the car accident, which happened in March of 1973 when I was 19 (are you doing the math? Have you figured out how old I am? The answer is 51 as of this date) is because I see that incident as the beginning of a very long and very slowly evolving downward spiral for me. So I thought I would use it as the start of an upward spiral for you and me together. I also feel the need to establish my bona fides with you right away, not unlike the aforementioned golf pro who clearly demonstrated his considerable skill from the outset. I guess I want you to know that for a very long span of time in my life, I was one monstrous mess. A spiritual, mental, and physical basket case with my head firmly planted where the sun does not shine. For a very long time my savior was whatever form of alcohol happened to be available, right up to and including the fateful day in June of 1983 that booze stopped working for me.

I also want to point out one of the things that I know I will be talking more about as this book evolves, because it is how I live my life: Anything that happens in our lives can be viewed from a number of different angles, some of them positive and some of them negative. The important thing to learn is that you can *always* choose the angle from which you view anything. *The choice is always yours.* I choose to look at the car accident as positive because it is the beginning of my downward spiral that eventually forced my upward spiral. The accident is also positive because it is something that can help to establish an understanding between us, a brotherhood of pain and misery as it were, that will enable us to more effectively communicate from heart to heart. I want you to know that I have most assuredly been there, done that. I have come out the other side with a sometimes fascinating assortment of experiences to use as tools for teaching. And devices for learning and teaching are all that mistakes are meant to be.

Chapter One - Choose Peace

The problem is where to begin. There is so much to say, so many stories to tell, and so much that I want to give you, so immediately and so completely that you never have to experience another moment of unhappiness! I want to be able to pour all there is, the whole enchilada, into one paragraph, with just the right words and in just such a way that you can instantaneously grasp everything and never again have to wonder if you will realize true and lasting happiness in your lifetime. It feels a little like trying to pour the entire Atlantic Ocean through the world's tiniest funnel and trying to decide which inch of shore line should go first.

However, as much as I think that giving you the whole thing immediately would be more fun than sinking a hole-in-one on a particularly difficult golf course (or any golf course for that matter) I do understand that such a thing is simply not possible from here. Neither I, nor any other human being possesses that kind of capability. The reason that neither I nor anyone else can impart to you a never-ending supply of love, peace, joy, and happiness is because they are already yours. They belong to you. You are already in possession of them. You came here with them, and they have not gone anywhere. My task is simply to help you to remember that which already exists inside you and always will. I can't provide you with the keys to the kingdom because they are already yours. I cannot give you anything you already have. I am simply going to show you where the keyhole is and prove to you, through the lens of my own experience, that the key is already in the lock, patiently waiting for you to give it a little turn.

All you need is sufficient *willingness* for just long enough so that you allow yourself to see just one new shred of truth. This will then give you the encouragement you need to keep going. You will find that moving along becomes a little less difficult and a little more pleasurable after a while. Whatever you do, do not stop. It simply is not worth it. The discomfort associated with growth and learning is nothing compared to the pain of living through the same old, same old, over and over again.

THE CHARACTERISTICS OF A LIFE BASED ON PEACE

Before we go much further it is important to make a certain point and make it very clearly: Choosing to live a life of peace is in no way an abdication. The peaceful position is not a position of weakness. It does not mean that you ever accept the un-acceptable. It does not mean that you lie down and allow people to roll over you. And it is not a position of "whatever". The position of peace is actually the most powerful one you can occupy. It is the greatest source of entirely grounded personal strength, emotional integrity, intellectual flexibility, and spiritual freedom. Unfortunately, you cannot know that unless you choose to go there. If you are feeling any amount of emotional turmoil, unhappiness, loss of control, crazy thinking, anguish, pain, frustration, anger, or fear in your life, choosing to go there would be a very good idea.

Learning to live a life of peace is a little bit like learning to scuba dive. You are initially excited about the possibility, but you are also a little bit terrified just before you take that first plunge into the water. You stand there with your mask all cleared and the regulator, that precious link to the life-sustaining tank of air you are carrying on your back, gripped firmly in your teeth, and you can't help but wonder what the hell you are doing here. At first you are somewhat tentative, moving slowly, convincing yourself that nothing terrible is going to happen and that you really can survive in this heretofore dark, forbidding, and unexplored environment. After you have actually inhaled and exhaled those first few breaths and you find that you still have a pulse and haven't been eaten by whatever denizens of the deep your overactive imagination can conjure, you begin to feel a little more comfortable. This strange and wonderful new comfort level is all you really need. It is the gateway to an entirely new and different world.

Once you pass through the gateway and allow yourself the freedom to hang around in your new environment long enough to experience a few of its wonders and delights, you find yourself involved in something that is so mind-boggling and all encompassing that finding the proper words to describe it is exceedingly difficult. Words indeed are entirely inadequate and unnecessary. As you take a moment every once in a while to look around at how incredibly well your life has unfolded as a result of choosing a path of peace, you will know that it is significantly better than you ever thought possible. And it will feel totally right to you.

You will know right down to the very depth of your heart and soul that it would never have happened if you hadn't made the original decision to allow it to happen, and then found the courage to step out of the way long enough to allow your Real Self to unfold. Once you get your first glimpse of the endless rewards that will always flow in your direction, you will understand that you are beginning to live a life that you previously only dreamed about. By natural extension then, fear of the future will begin to disappear because you can look forward and know that what will happen to you is much greater than your greatest dream today. Imagine looking into the future and feeling excited rather than terrified! All you have to do is make a decision, a real commitment to that decision, then simply get out of the way and let it be handled for you.

One of the things that you will find as an undercurrent in this book is that any skill you learn in one aspect of your life can be used to good purpose in every other aspect of your life as well. This is because everything works according to the same principles. The form may seem to be dramatically different,

Chapter One - Choose Peace

but in substance it is all the same. If a new way of thinking or behaving works in the office, then it will work at home.

For instance, I realize that for me writing this book is a microcosm of essentially how I have grown to live my life. I recognized my need to write this book because it brings me closer to becoming the person God originally intended for me to be. But still, I get to decide. Writing or not writing is my decision. I get to choose what I do and what I think. I could decide I have better ways to spend my time and go about doing those things instead. But this book would be talking to me every day, calling me to it, and there is nothing I can do to change that. Therefore, deciding not to write would cause me the sort of discomfort that always occurs when we do not think and behave in ways that accurately reflect who we really are.

So I decided to write, and having made the decision, I have made a commitment to the decision because it is the right thing for me to do. Having made a decision and a commitment to the decision, the deal is done. Now the only thing I need to do is become willing to step out of the way and allow the words to come *through* me rather than from me. Yes, I am sitting in front of my laptop and I am typing the words, but they are not my words. They are coming from the same place that provides us all the breath of life. Oftentimes I look at the screen and wonder where those words came from because they most assuredly did not come from me.

The point is that once a decision and commitment is made, all you have to do is get out of the way and become willing because everything will be taken care of for you.

So I get to have fun on this side of the book, and you get to have your fun on your side of the book. And we will both learn a great deal along the way. Also, I really do know that writing this book and sharing my journey with you is part of the process of becoming the person that God originally intended me to be. And because you are here with me this far, it is now part of your process as well.

Chapter One - Choose Peace

THE GOOD NEWS AND THE BAD NEWS

Some of what I have learned is this:

Peace is inevitable.

Pain and suffering are entirely optional.

The choice is yours.

That's right, you actually do get to choose. You get to pick the greatest Grand Prize you could ever possibly hope to imagine, a prize so magnificent that winning ten lotteries on the very same day could never bring you the riches and abundance that choosing a life of peace can bring. I know this to be true because I have done it. I have done it and continue to do it every day of my life and there isn't any question that it actually works.

I once read a book by Peter McWilliams called *You Can't Afford The Luxury Of A Negative Thought,* a book that I would highly recommend reading. In discussing how we decide that which is really within the realm of possibility for us, McWilliams points out in a very pragmatic way that if anyone else has ever done it, then you can do it, too. He goes on to say that if nobody else has ever done something that you want to do, then you can be the first. Essentially, this means that you can achieve anything you want as long as you make the decision to go for it and then make a commitment to that decision, no matter what.

I can absolutely assure you, beyond the shadow of a doubt, that I am not the first person in human history to choose peace, and I will not be the last. Those who have chosen have reaped rewards that are entirely free and eminently available to anyone, yourself included.

So take a few minutes, sit down with yourself in a quiet place, and look at your life. Ask yourself some questions. Does what you see reflect love, joy, compassion, generosity, and harmony in a pain-free, nourishing, and stressless environment? Or do you see and feel anger, fear, turmoil, and resentment, in an environment of difficulties and pain. Do you see problems, or do you see only solutions? Do you react to life's circumstances and situations, trying to do the best you can and feeling more often than not that it just isn't good enough? Or do you actively initiate your life and innately know that everything always works out right? Is life a struggle or does it just flow? Are you constantly judging yourself and others, or do you accept yourself and others unconditionally? Are you always smiling and laughing on the inside as well as the outside, or do you mostly feel like crawling under a rock and hiding from everyone and everything? Are you always entirely comfortable in your own skin, or do you often wonder who and what you really are? Do you have a lot of crazy thoughts that you never want to let see the light of day and which make you think there is something seriously wrong with you? Or are you able to laugh at the nutty stuff that sometimes goes in and out of your head, enjoying the show for whatever it might be?

As you ask yourself these questions and any others that happen to come to your mind, please remember that you have the ability and the power to choose. It is not necessary to live in doubt and fear. You have not been condemned to live a painful and difficult life because you have made some mistakes in the past. You are not a bad person or a sinner because you have done some things or thought some things that you currently wish you hadn't. Quite the contrary. The only value that your

Chapter One - Choose Peace

past has for you now is that it has taken everything that has occurred in your life to get you where you are today. Right now your slate is clean, and you can learn to make different choices which will most assuredly lead to different results. Remember:

Peace is inevitable.

Pain and suffering are entirely optional.

The choice is yours.

This is the absolute truth. It is also both the good news and the bad news.

It is the good news in that the kind of life of which you have always dreamed, the life that is full of love, happiness, joy, peace, serenity, and abundance, really is yours for the choosing. Imagine living a life where you know right down to the bottom of your being that no matter what decision you make in any given situation, you cannot make a wrong choice. Imagine the freedom of being able to decide - for yourself - what is best for you and not worrying about the million or so ramifications of your choice because you completely understand that if it is the best thing for you, then it is the best thing for everyone else as well. Imagine the strength you will feel when you finally understand that there isn't anything anyone can do or say that can hurt you in any way without you deciding to allow yourself to be hurt. And imagine waking up every morning to face the new day without a feeling of anxiety, fear, dread, nervousness, or trepidation of any sort, where waking up in the morning is nothing more than a simple transition from sleeping to wakefulness.

HOW TO ENJOY PEACE IN YOUR LIFE EVERY DAY

Here's the bad news: making a choice for peace will bring an end to the seemingly endless parade of emotionally charged situations in your life that at least provide you with something to do, something to talk about, a way to get the attention we all so very much crave and seem to need, something that is familiar to focus on, and a way to feel uniquely important. Let's face it: If the universe has singled you out as the one upon whom one pile of shit after another must get heaped, then you must really be important. Although you may not think of it in quite this way, you must admit the pain, anger, fear, anxiety, upset, and generally negative feelings that you say you would love to get rid of are at least familiar to you and actually appear to have a life of their own. They sort of come in and go out of their own accord, constantly chipping away at you and beating you down like the action of a relentless sea forever attacking and eroding an all-too-delicate stretch of pristine shore.

The familiarity of pain can often be more compelling than the initial and paradoxical discomfort experienced when the pain is eliminated.

Choosing a life of peace and giving up all the negativity and attendant drama that currently fills many of your waking moments will be like giving up your best friend. What would you do with yourself if you had nothing to complain about? What kinds of things could possibly occupy your mind and your thoughts if you weren't constantly worried about situations like not having enough money, being stuck in yet another relationship that is full of constant fighting and disagreement, or having a family that just doesn't get it and is always trying to push your buttons. How sick of it all you are! When is the world finally going to give you a break anyway? How would you ever recognize yourself if the future had no immi-

Chapter One - Choose Peace

nent disaster lurking around every corner because disaster is all there has ever been?

Once you begin to remove the cloud of guilt, remorse, anger, fear, doubt, and insecurity - whether it is bit by precious bit or in massive ugly chunks - and you begin to behave and feel differently, you will perceive that your entire world will be changing as well. And so it will. The world you look at every day will begin to appear differently to you. It will appear as though it is changing because it will be reflecting back to you the changes you are making inside. This can be a little disconcerting at first because it is new and different. You have become used to doing business in a certain way, and even if it isn't any fun, it is still the devil you know as opposed to the devil you don't know.

Chapter One - Choose Pe

CHOOSING PEACE CONNECTS YOU TO YOUR REAL SELF

Beginning to live a life where peace is the drug of choice often leaves you with the feeling that the demon you used to know is now sneaking up on you from behind and looking to take a huge bite out of your butt. At this point it is fairly normal to begin to have doubts and to wonder if there was really anything wrong with you to begin with. A more effective and appropriate line of thinking would be to consider what is now *right* with you. If you are ever wondering whether or not something is going to return, doesn't that mean that it is currently gone? And isn't that the goal?

I know it sounds a little ridiculous. Choosing between a life where everyone or everything else is a rock-solid pain in the ass on the one hand, or a life of understanding that there isn't anything anyone else can do or say that can touch the person you really are and always have been would certainly seem to be rather easy. Isn't it easy to decide between living a life where, if it weren't for the incredibly stupid and thoughtless things other people say and do you wouldn't have any problems at all, or to simply focus on yourself so everything will work out significantly better than your most fantastic dreams?

I know, I know. You're asking me how I could possibly think that, given the choice, I could ever imagine anyone choosing to keep living life from one dysfunctional relationship to the next, constantly looking for, and never finding, that one right person with whom to blissfully spend the remainder of their days? How could I imagine that anyone would actually *choose* to keep getting out of bed every day with their head and heart immediately consumed by the constant buzzing of all those negative thoughts and emotions that, try as they might, they have never been able to successfully get rid of for any appreciable length of time? How could I ever imagine that anyone could possibly choose to keep worrying about whether or not they are going to have enough money to pay the bills and put the proper amount of food on the table?

It is because I have seen many people choose the prison of the familiar over the exhilarating freedom of letting go.

I have certainly been there, done that. I stood at the crossroads. I made my choice. And then I had to engage every ounce of personal discipline and determination I could find to make myself keep going when giving up would have been much easier. But giving up is easier only in the short term and only in terms of effort expended. Giving up and choosing the familiarity of guilt and fear over the unknown possibility of personal peace and unconditional love is monumentally more difficult in the long run. Of course, you can't know that until you experience it. And in order for you to get there, perhaps it would be helpful for you to hear from someone who has looked at the same wall that is currently standing before you, someone who made the choice for unlimited life and found a way to walk around the wall rather than go right through it.

I began this book with the story of that particular car accident (there were a number of others as well) because I wanted you to know that I have walked through the valley of the shadow of death. I made the choice for peace in my life, I have made an irrevocable commitment to that choice, and now the valley does not even exist. I also know today that the valley and the wall only existed in my mind. They weren't real; I made them up. And if I can do it, so can you. There is nothing special about me.

Chapter One - Choose Peace

The reason you can make your choice - and by making a commitment to your choice, actually attain all the peace, love, decency, dignity, compassion, generosity, and freedom that you could ever hope to imagine - is because those things are already yours. You just don't know it. Making the choice simply opens the connections to that which already exists. It is akin to when the first telephone lines were laid down so that people in New York could talk directly to people in Chicago. It isn't that these places did not exist prior to the telephone lines being laid down; it was simply that the line connecting the two cities did not exist. In your case it is actually much easier, because the line that connects you directly to your Real Self already exists. It always has and always will. You simply lack the experience of actually using it. You have merely forgotten that the line is already there and the handset is sitting in the cradle, patiently waiting for you to pick it up and come home.

Deciding to live a life of personal peace puts the handset squarely in your hand and places it ever so gently against your ear.

The fact is that you have always had a choice and you have always opted for the turmoil, upheaval, and unrest because you didn't know that another avenue was available to you. And you didn't know that you didn't know. Even if you do not look at all troubled or disturbed to any outside observer, the truth is that you feel it on the inside. You have developed considerable skill at hiding just how lousy you very often feel and have become rather accustomed to talking about anything and everything except that which is of the most importance to you.

It is much safer and certainly more fashionable to be as shallow as possible. It is hard work to actually think your way through the layers of bullshit you like to tell yourself that keep you from taking risks. You can decide to put this book away, throw it in the trash, conduct a ritual incineration with it in your fireplace, or perhaps freely give it to someone you really do not like so that it can make *them* crazy instead of you. But doing that would do nothing for you, and you know it. Or you can keep reading and begin the process of deciding how you are going to *live your life* rather than letting what you think and do be dictated by decidedly unfriendly and unsympathetic outside forces.

Chapter One - Choose Peace

ONE MAN'S DECISION IS STRONGER THAN AN ARMY

Viktor Frankl was an eminent Austrian psychologist who had the unfortunate circumstance of living in Austria at the same time the Nazis decided to "annex" the country. Frankl's misfortune was compounded by the fact that he also happened to be Jewish, and one of the ways the Nazis helped themselves to the illusion of superiority was by creating the myth of the inferiority of other races. Whether we are talking about nations, races, religions, or individual people, anybody wishing to make themselves feel superior in any way, must first find another nation, race, religion, or individual to cast in the role of inferior entity. If something or someone else is inferior to me, or sub-human as the Nazis used to say, then it naturally follows that I must be superior.

In order for one to be true, the other must be true. But it is all a colossal lie. If we, as a nation or individuals, are trying to build ourselves up by putting others down, we *always* succeed in doing neither because this entire line of thinking and behaving is based on lies. Lies by their very nature are not grounded in reality, are entirely fleeting, and can never survive the light of rigorous and thorough thought and examination. They simply cannot stand up to the tests of time and scrutiny.

A lie is a lie. Bullshit is bullshit. And lasting good can never evolve from lies because a real foundation does not exist underneath the lies. You can rest assured that the house of cards must eventually come tumbling down.

It wasn't long after the Nazis invaded that they began to act like Nazis and round up all the Jews, Gypsies, Communists, homosexuals, and any other entire class of people they did not think measured up to their ideal standard of the master race. A short life of forced slave labor in a network of unimaginable concentration camps seemed to be a good idea for the hundreds of thousands of people who were collected and carted off. It cost the Reich virtually nothing to run the camps and the sheer economic value of all that free labor contributed mightily to the German's ability to wage war. So what if the prisoners died by the train load? This was a good thing as far as the Nazis were concerned because a new train load was always available to take their place, and the general population of all these undesirable people was steadily diminishing.

But the population was not diminishing fast enough for the likes of Hitler and Eichmann, so they devised the "Final Solution" of extermination camps to hasten the process. Places like Auschwitz and Dachau became the terminus for masses of humanity and places of unconscionable horror and human degradation. The skeletons of these camps stand today as monuments to man's ability and willingness to destroy man. Viktor Frankl spent many years of unfathomable hardship and suffering in these most infamous examples of man's ability to be cruel to himself.

Yet he survived. And went on to write a book about why he survived and why others, who were obviously stronger and more fit than he was, did not live to see the end of the war. *Man's Search For Meaning* is one of the most powerful and inspirational books I have ever read. I would highly recommend it to anyone wishing to learn some extraordinarily valuable lessons as to what is important and what is not. Frankl had the ability as a trained psychologist to remove himself from center stage, so to speak, and to take an objective look at his life and his camp experience. His book is not a compendium of outrage after outrage that denounces the fiendish

Chapter One - Choose Peace

Germans and extol his own virtue. Rather, it is more of a detached examination of what really happened and how it was that he came out the other side a whole man.

One of the things that became most clear to him was that he had a reason to live. He was convinced that he had not accomplished all that he was sent here to accomplish. He was also very much in love with his wife and he was determined to be reunited with her. Love is that what sustained him, and having a reason to live gave him the strength to go on and endure to the end.

Also - and for the purposes of my book this is the most important part - Frankl came to the realization of an extraordinarily astounding fact. He discovered that "the last of the human freedoms is the ability to choose our own attitude." Because it is too easy to read this quote and go scurrying past it without giving it the attention it deserves, I will say it again.

"The last of the human freedoms is the ability to choose our own attitude."

Think about that for a moment. What Frankl is saying is that we have the freedom to choose our own attitude about everything that happens in our lives. We have been given the freedom to decide exactly what we think and how we feel about everything that happens to us. It is one of our birthrights. In Frankl's camp experience the most common and acceptable way for the inmates to see themselves was in the role of helpless victim. Everything in their lives, including whether they lived or died, was being decided for them by people whom they saw as having ultimate power over them. Circumstances outside themselves and well beyond their control therefore determined how they felt on the inside. It is this very desperation that led many of the inmates to simply give up and accept death as the only way to put an end to their physical suffering. For many, it became the only way out of the camps.

In a very real sense the camp guards did have the power to kill any inmate whenever the spirit moved them, clearly knowing there would be no repercussions. The guards and the camp authorities could commit one atrocity after another upon the body of whatever inmate happened to be in front of them, whenever the mood struck, and such behavior was entirely accepted, condoned, and applauded. However, Frankl began to understand that while the guards did have power over his body, the mind did not necessarily have to follow. His body was not his mind.

Frankl had found another way. He had found a way that most of us spend entire lifetimes constantly chasing and never catching. Once he decided that he, *and only he,* could choose his own perspective, that he and not the guards was in charge of what he thought and how he felt, that only he had the power over how he would view everything that happened to him and others in the camps every day, that he had the freedom to choose his own attitude and would not allow his attitude to be chosen for him, then the Nazis could not touch him. They could bring untold misery upon his body and physically hurt him in many ways, but they could not touch his spirit. They did not have control over his mind. They did not determine how he would think or what he would think about. They could neither determine his reactions nor cower him with threats. They could not touch him. His body might have been at effect of the Nazis but his mind was his own.

Incredible!

Chapter One - Choose Peace

The power of one mind firmly standing on a foundation of love rather than fear was more powerful than the combined physical might of the entire German Army.

Astounding!

Viktor Frankl found freedom in the midst of one of the most unspeakable horrors in human history. He discovered the abject strength and unlimited power that only love can provide. He picked up the handset on his end of the line and connected to that which was already his. He found peace in the middle of absolute chaos. The question then beckons: If he can do it there, why can't we do it here, where our lives are relative cakewalks? The answer is that of course we can. The problem is that we do not know that freedom, peace, love, joy, serenity, and harmony are already ours, always have been and always will be. Nobody ever told us that all we have to do is remove the blocks to this perfect peace that we have unwittingly constructed over the course of our lives, and we will have it in endless abundance.

Imagine the possibilities! Imagine the freedom you will feel when you finally *know* that no matter what seems to be going wrong in your life, no matter what kind of shitstorm seems to be coming down around your ears, no matter how much other people seem to be not getting it, *nothing can touch you!* This, folks, is well worth the proverbial price of admission.

Frankl was able to put his ego aside long enough to allow himself to reconnect to the love with which he was originally created. Love cannot be touched, changed, altered, manipulated or manufactured by man because it was not made by man. Love is what we are. But it is not of us. We are of love. The sense of peace we so longingly search for in our lives is a natural extension of the love that created us. In order to experience this peace, our job is simply to choose it. Choose it and commit to it over all else, and it will be yours. Every day. For the rest of your life.

There are no exceptions to this rule.

Chapter One - Choose Peace

MY CHOICE FOR PEACE

You really do get to make the choice and the truth is that you have already chosen. You just do not know that you have chosen everything that has occurred in your life up to this point. You do not need to agree with me about that right now. I wouldn't expect you to be able to do so because it is quite a leap from conventional thinking. Yet it is precisely the conventional, default type of thinking that we will be seeking to eliminate from your life in the time we spend together. It is that kind of thinking that gets in the way of experiencing the peace and love which are just sitting there waiting for you. Yes, you can choose love instead of fear, peace instead of turmoil, contentment rather than upset, freedom rather than guilt, self acceptance rather than shame, and wholeness rather than emptiness.

I currently own a small printing business approximately 25 minutes north of Boston. I once had a woman who worked for me in a customer-service position who was exceptionally good at what she did. She had been in the printing business for a very long time and had an intrinsic understanding of the process. Molly (I changed the name out of respect for her) could do more work and stay on top of more details than at least two or three other people. I purposely stayed out of the way of her developing relationships with our customers because we are in a business where relationships and connections go a long way. In fact, I encouraged her to spend time with our most important clients.

Over time, Molly's life became more and more out of control. She was always getting herself into one jam after another: Speeding tickets, loss of drivers license, time out of work for various and sundry personal problems, and a serious drug and alcohol dependency with all of the attendant drama became a way of life for her over time. I paid her extremely well, most of which unfortunately found its way up her nose. But she still worked like a dog, and the customers loved her. They thought that she and her personal foibles were very funny and superbly entertaining.

I was very reluctant to let her go for a number of reasons. The first one is the most obvious. I was afraid that I would have a very difficult time finding a replacement with her caliber of knowledge and experience. The second is that I was afraid she would go to work for a competitor and take with her many of the customers with whom I encouraged her to develop a relationship. Clearly, this would weaken the business and diminish my own personal income. Also, I was of the mistaken belief that I could eventually find the right words to say to her that would finally make a difference. I thought that if I paid her enough money, or kept changing my attitude toward her, or continued to ignore all of the data that was right before my eyes regarding the exact nature of the problem, everything would eventually work itself out.

Sound familiar?

The problem was that while she was great from the customer point of view, she was absolutely miserable to work with. Her language was foul and offensive and her attitude was poisonous. Her first and only concern was herself, and she didn't give a rat's ass about anything or anybody else. Her main concern was, "What's in it for me?" Every other employee hated to work with her and always walked on eggshells around her. Nobody wanted to incur Molly's wrath.

As for me, I actually hated going to my own office. I started to get queasy feelings in the pit of my stomach and a slight

Chapter One - Choose Peace

pounding inside my head whenever I started to drive in the direction of my own company. I literally could not stand being in the same room with her and avoided asking her to come into my personal office for any reason. I always avoided having an employee cookout at my house in the summertime because I refused to have my children come in contact with Molly in any way. Yet she continued to make me a lot of money, which I generously shared with her.

I was afraid to let her go. I came close on a number of occasions, but I always backed away because I was afraid of the repercussions. I was afraid it would cripple my business. I was afraid that I would never be able to find an adequate replacement, I was afraid that it would look like a sign of weakness, and I was afraid that I couldn't handle it. Also, I knew that I was at least in part responsible for creating the monster, and I felt a lot of guilt, shame, and inadequacy around that. But the bottom line is that I was just plain scared. Fear, not Molly, was the only problem I had.

But then one day something happened, and I can't even remember exactly what it was. All I remember is that it was relatively small. But it became the proverbial straw that broke the camel's back. What I do remember is that I made a clear-cut decision that changed my life forever in ways that I never would have been able to predict.

I decided that, no matter what, I was going to have peace. I hated how I felt going to my office, and I couldn't stand how everyone was being affected. I decided that peace was more important to me than money, and I was going to have peace in my office no matter what. If I had to lose every single customer I had and every single one of my employees, if I had to start my business all over again completely by myself from scratch, I was absolutely willing to do it. Ramifications and details were no longer important. I was no longer concerned with what might or might not happen. I decided that I would have peace in my office. I decided that I owed it to myself and every single one of my employees to create a peaceful working atmosphere and to never, ever, compromise on that issue. And so I did.

After having made my decision, I fired Molly first thing the next morning, just as sure as I am sitting here typing away on my trusty little laptop. But it is important to make one thing perfectly clear, as Richard Nixon used to say. My decision was not about whether or not to fire Molly. My decision was only about having peace in my office. Firing Molly was a natural extension of the decision for peace. This is a very important distinction.

You see, simply firing Molly would not really have changed anything for me. According to this dynamic, I would have seen her as the problem and I would have seen firing her as the obvious solution. I would then have been shocked when I eventually hired someone just like Molly and ended up in the same position, wondering why I always seemed to attract all the fruitcakes. I would have learned nothing, and nothing would have changed. If you are ever wondering why the same kind of shit keeps occurring over and over again in your life (same book different cover) look in the mirror.

I had to recognize that my problem had nothing to do with Molly. She was just a symbol, an outward manifestation of that which was going on inside me. The only problem I had was myself and the choices I was making, the compromises I was making with my own integrity, the rationalizations I was willing to make and actually listen to, the crap I was willing to

Chapter One - Choose Peace

accept from one person and nobody else. I was the one who allowed her to assume the "special" and "untouchable" status in my office. If anyone else behaved toward me and the other people in the office the way Molly did, they would have been immediately thrown out without a second thought.

I had created the monster, and the only way to drive a wooden stake through it's ugly heart was to look in the mirror and understand that I have met the enemy - and the enemy is me. Of course, I had had talks with her about what was acceptable and what was not acceptable, and everything would be just fine for some period of time. Eventually, however, we would be right back to business as usual, and I would allow it to go on until we reached a point of critical mass and had to have another chat. But nothing changed because nothing changed.

I needed to make the change in me. I needed to decide that inner peace was exactly what I was going to have before I could start attracting all the things into my life which would reflect back to me such a decision and state of mind. I needed to find a place to stand and make a decision to stand there, come what may. Sure I was scared, downright terrified. But the only way to overcome unreasonable fear (and all fear is unreasonable, which we will eventually get to) is to walk right up to it, kick it in the balls, and boldly do that which frightens you the most.

So the decision I made was not about changing the situation in which I was involved. This would only have granted me a temporary reprieve until the next Molly came along for my learning pleasure. Had I gone about it that way, I would essentially have been trying to change the world outside of myself in order to change the world inside, and this can *never* work. It can *never* work. The decision I made was about changing my life and the only way to do that is to change from the inside to the outside because the outer world, the world we see, is *always* a reflection of that which is occurring on the inside. It is *always* a reflection of that which is occurring on the inside. We will be discussing this in greater detail later in the book.

God, there is just so much to get to!

Since then, every business decision I have ever made has had the maintenance and growing of an atmosphere of peace and personal safety in my office as a central factor. I don't imagine I will be changing that any time in the near future. It is just too much fun!

I have learned much from having made my initial decision for peace. One of the most interesting things is that while my original choice for peace really had to do with my business, I actually ended up applying it to every aspect of my life. I had no idea that I was making a decision that really had to do with my entire life, I thought it was strictly a business decision. I found out that what I do in one place I certainly do at least a variation of everywhere I go. Wherever you go, there you are. Over the past few years I have learned much about achieving peace as well as the excuses we can convincingly fabricate to keep ourselves from making the choice - or having made the choice, that which we are capable of doing in order to keep ourselves from following through. And all of this is what I seek to share with you through the vehicle of this book. Remember;

Peace is inevitable.

Pain and suffering are optional.

The choice is yours.

Chapter One - Choose Peace

<u>YOU WILL KNOW PEACE AND SERENITY</u>

You will experience peace. There is no way to get around that fact. Love is your source, your first cause, so to speak, and peace is an inherent aspect of the love that created you long before you took your first breath. You will always return to love because it is what you are, and you can no more change that than you can make the Boston Red Sox win a World Series title. (Author's note: I began this book long before the unbelievable triumph of the Boston Red Sox in the 2004 World Series. I decided to keep that line in the book, however, for the sake of nostalgia.) The choice that you are currently being asked to make is whether you want to experience a peaceful, joyful, loving life, or whether you would like to wait until you give up your physical body in order to have such an experience. You can have it now or you can have it later, but have it you will.

You can connect to the love and peace which is your birthright starting now, or you can put the decision off and have all the pain, frustration, anger, and fear that your heart desires for the time being. Peace is yours for the choosing because peace is what you are. And it feels a whole lot better to be connected to who you really are than not. At least this is my experience and the experience of many other people I know who have chosen to follow a similar path.

The human race will experience peace because peace is a fundamental aspect of the love that created and sustains us, a love that is eternal, a love that is not of man but of God. If you have a problem with the concept of "God,", you can substitute any one of many different concepts such as: "The Universal Force For Good," Allah, Buddha, Yahweh, Higher Power, Supreme Being, anything you like. The point is that the love and peace which is the essence of whatever concept you decide to latch onto existed long before man drew his first breath and will continue long after life as we know it ceases to exist. Love is as eternal as is God because love and God are one and the same.

In as much as anything you create is an extension of you - be it a painting, a book, a sculpture, a sand castle, or a family - you are an extension of the eternal love that created you. Your creation can no more separate itself from you as its author or source than you can successfully separate yourself from your source. You are perfectly free to deny that you have been created as a loving extension and critical part of that which I call God and which you are free to call anything you like. Such a choice merely delays the inevitable and allows you to maintain the illusion of your own power and control. Such a choice also guarantees that you will live your life in a significantly more limited and restricted manner than would otherwise be possible, and you may not even know it.

This is as true as true can be and there is nothing you can do about it. You can deny it, choose to ignore it, burn this book and invoke your right to be an atheist, having nothing remotely to do with any concept that invokes the dreaded "G word." But there is nothing you can do to change the one irrevocable fact that you were created by love, and love is what you are. You have simply forgotten the true nature of your Real Self, and all you really need to do is remember. I know this to be true because I have lived the experience and there is nothing special about me.

So the first step in our journey together is to notice the need for internal peace and happiness. This is usually facilitated by first noticing the lack of peace, harmony, love, and serenity.

Chapter One - Choose Peace

The next step is to choose to have a greater sense of peace and possibility in your life. Make a conscious decision to pick up the handset on your end of the line and connect to the Real Power in your life. This is all you need to do right now, and your life will change in ways that will astound you.

Go ahead, make your choice.

CHAPTER TWO

MAKE A COMMITMENT

Chapter Two - Make A Commitment To Your Choice

"Death is not the greatest loss in life. The greatest loss is what dies inside us as we live."

- Norman Cousins

"No one can fail who seeks to reach the truth."

- A Course In Miracles

"Until one is committed, there is hesitancy, the chance to draw back, always ineffectiveness. Concerning all acts of initiative (and creation) there is one elementary truth, the ignorance of which kills countless ideas and splendid plans: That the moment one definitely commits oneself, then Providence moves too. All sorts of things occur to help one that would never otherwise have occurred. A whole stream of events issues from the decision, raising in one's favor all manner of unforeseen incidents and meetings and material assistance, which no man could have dreamed would have come his way. I have learned a deep respect for one of Goethe's couplets:

"Whatever you can do,
    or dream you can, begin it.
        Boldness has genius,
            Power, and magic in it."

- W. H. Murray
The Scottish Himalayan Expedition

Chapter Two - Make A Commitment To Your Choice

THE MEMORABLE DATE

The setting sun burned a bright reddish orange hole in the progressively darkening sky. The air was getting cooler and the waning rays of the sun no longer provided the luxurious warmth, cozy feelings of security, and abiding awareness that everything is as it ought to be. Fleeting sparks of reflected light could still be seen dancing across the choppy surface of the languid river some 25 stories below. The once massively polluted and now becoming cleaner by the day waters of the Charles River moved lazily from the northwest to the southeast, effectively separating the bastion of history that is the City of Boston from the mother lode of intellectual and social snobbery that is the City of Cambridge.

The river completes its ancient journey in the also once massively polluted Boston Harbor which is now getting cleaned up thanks to billions of dollars invested in a sewage treatment plant that actually works. The Chaahles, as any native Bostonian calls the river, is lined on both sides by a string of what look to be evenly spaced trees, no doubt the inspired brainchild of someone's urban planning project. From where I sat, the trees looked like they were bursting at the seams with leaves that had morphed into the bright splashes of red, orange, and yellow that will always conjure images of fall in New England. They looked like small and fluffy balls of colored cotton yarn from my vantage point high above the river, and they were yet another reminder of the reality of the changing seasons. The rhythm of life in New England revolves around and is dictated by the peculiarities of the seasons. It is a little like living four distinctly short years within the context of one long one.

The stifling hot dog days of summer generally mean golf, Red

Sox baseball, swimming in whatever body of water is available and sufficiently clean for such accommodation, and freedom from school. The fall brings with it the clear, clean, and crisply refreshing cool air that always smells like the return of the school year and fosters a shift in focus to football, hockey, basketball, hiking, and raking the leaves that so dutifully fall to the ground. The sometimes bleak and dark feel of the too-long winters means shorter days and messy snowfalls. It means shoveling off the walkway and plowing the driveway and massive traffic jams whenever the forecast even hints at the possibility of a major storm. It also means that panic-stricken crowds descend on every available supermarket whenever a storm is predicted, as though we lived in a remote corner of the barren wastes of Siberia and food would not be available for the next 106 years.

With the arrival of spring we move the clocks ahead one hour while the promise of new life and love is reflected in the lengthening daylight as well as the pure delight (or is it just plain relief?) you feel when you glimpse those first crocuses and daffodils poking themselves out of what must be still cold and unfriendly ground. Spring is a time of renewal, a time to lighten one's heart and celebrate the sheer joy of having survived yet another dark and depressing winter. How could people ever live in places like Iceland, Greenland, Finland, or Norway, where the reassuring rays of a life-giving sun cannot be seen for months at a time?

Sitting at my window-side table in the Spinnaker restaurant on the Cambridge side of the river afforded a view of the Boston skyline that is without a doubt the best there is. The somewhat pregnant rise of Beacon Hill in the midst of all those marvels of construction lends a charming and antique sense of character to the city that is nicknamed "The Hub" because it

Chapter Two - Make A Commitment To Your Choice

was once considered the hub of the universe. Boston, my home town, is a city dripping with history and political intrigue, an incredible mixture of architectural styles well forged in the fickle cauldron of time gone by, a place where important decisions are made, and blue-blooded Boston Brahmins continue to sincerely believe that the universe revolves inexorably around them.

The Spinnaker restaurant is perched on top of The Hyatt Regency Hotel and boasts a slowly moving floor that completely revolves once every hour and which affords its patrons a 180 degree easterly view of the river and the city that is incomparable. I sat there in my ever-so-slowly moving seat, looking out at the magnificent view, and I couldn't have cared less. None of it made a damn bit of difference to me. Not the view, not the color of the sun, not the long and interesting history of the City of Boston, nor the magnificent skyline that at times seemed so close that I felt like I could reach out and touch it. No, I didn't give a rat's ass about blue blooded Brahmins. I couldn't have cared less about the changing seasons or whether the Celtics enjoyed still another championship year. Nothing could penetrate, nothing could touch the heart that had once been so sensitive but was now deeply buried under the rubble of too many conflicting and unresolved emotions. I simply did not care. I could not care. I was unable to care.

I wanted to care. My God I wanted to care, but I somehow seemed to have lost the ability and capacity for such sentiments which really only succeeded in making me that much more vulnerable. I once had cared, that much I knew, because I remembered having been a very sensitive young boy. Yet now I was a grown man and I didn't particularly give a shit that I was here, sitting at a window seat in a revolving restaurant on the top floor of the Hyatt Regency with a view to die for, meeting another in a string of blind dates that I was absolutely certain would amount to nothing, being totally beyond the ability to feel real joy or happiness about anything. I just wanted to get through this night as soon as possible and get on with living my miserable and lonely existence, thank you very much.

I had chosen The Spinnaker because it looked good on the outside, which was very important to me. Making such a choice reflected a certain amount of good taste and accomplishment, don't you know. In my mind, or what was left of it at the time, this choice somehow reflected a modicum of success. After all, it wasn't The Tam Tavern located in the bowels of Boston's Combat Zone that served twenty five cent drafties and was populated by ragged drunks drooling all over themselves when they weren't too busy puking poison all over the floors and tables. I did show a little style and character with my selection of meeting venues, and I probably looked ok in my clean suit, starched white shirt, and shined shoes.

Yes, I had become fairly adept at looking good on the outside while I continued to rapidly deteriorate on the inside. Just how far can someone deteriorate until there is no more deterioration left, when you have hit the very bottom and there is no more down? What happens then? It scared the living bejeezus out of me to think that I would probably find out one fine and sunny day. So, I had to keep moving, keep planning, keep executing the plan, keep my bags packed and my running shoes all laced up, because the last thing in the world I wanted to do was stop and catch up to myself. I was scared to death of what such an encounter might reveal.

In the meantime, I couldn't let on to anyone that I was just

Chapter Two - Make A Commitment To Your Choice

about certifiably out of my mind. So I had to look good and mind my manners, when what I really felt like doing, more often than not, was scratch someone's eyes out.

I can't remember if she was a blond or a redhead, nor can I recall her name, and it really does not matter. Actually, I am beginning to think that this was actually the second time I met this particular woman, one of the very few with whom an encore performance was granted or tolerated, depending on your perspective. The one thing I do remember, however, is that I somehow became fixated on the question of who was going to pick up the tab.

For some reason, known only to the deepest, darkest part of my fear-driven ego, the only thing I could think about was whether or not she was going to offer to pay for our drinks. I didn't hear a word she said because I had become so fixated on this question of the drink tab. I am quite certain I decided almost immediately that she was going to leave the bill with me, and I began to build a resentment right away. Now, the entire bill probably amounted to somewhere in the vicinity of fourteen dollars because we were just having a drink or two and were not having dinner, so the amount of money in question was totally insignificant. It wasn't about the money and I knew it. But I couldn't let it go. I tried. I knew it made no sense. Yet I was entirely incapable of putting this newest bit of insanity aside long enough to enjoy even a particle of the conversation. I really had to work my ass off to keep myself contained because the last thing in the world I wanted was to let on that there was anything wrong with me. I certainly did not want her to know exactly what I was thinking.

Of course, she was probably quite relieved when the time came to go along on our separate ways. God knows she had good reason to wonder what kind of nut she just spent a couple of hours with, and I am sure she began to pray that I would never call her again.

So, it doesn't take a rocket scientist, a tremendous leap of creative imagination, or does it take an energetic flight of fancy to figure out that I had a very difficult time establishing any kind of an intimate relationship with a woman. Truth be told, I had a hard time establishing relationships with anyone at all. Like I said, what you do in one place you certainly do at least a variation on that theme everywhere you go, whether you know it or not. Also, the world you see outside yourself is really only a reflection of the world that exists inside you. This is something that we will discuss in greater detail later. But for the purposes of this discussion, if the outside world was reflecting back to me my own perception of the insanity that clearly existed on the inside, it is no wonder I wanted to keep running and hiding. This would have made for one very terrifying place.

I wanted to share the story of this date because it is a good representation of where I was mentally, emotionally, and spiritually at the time. In terms of chronology, this event happened about halfway through the part of my life I refer to as the dry-drunk phase. The dry-drunk phase lasted about six and a half years so that by the time I reached the end of it I was significantly worse off than I was when I met the redhead (or was she a blond?) at the Hyatt. I eventually became a certifiable basket case.

Chapter Two - Make A Commitment To Your Choice

PUTTING DOWN THE DRINK

In order for someone to become a dry drunk, he or she must first become a wet one.

For approximately 14 years, from the age of sixteen to thirty, I hid from relationships and just about everything else under a river of alcohol. I was not consciously aware of the fact that my life was driven by fear and that I was looking to a bottle of booze to assuage my fear and provide me with the courage I needed to face life. I also understand today that it is not uncommon for people to turn to things like alcohol, drugs, gambling, sex, television, movies, or food to provide some sort of relief from the emotional trap that fear builds around the heart.

If you had asked me during those turbulent years, I would have told you quite confidently and rather convincingly that friends was something I had in plentiful supply. I most likely even believed that bullshit myself! In fact, any objective outside observer would have seen me as a fairly energetic, outgoing, confident, and successful individual. But if alcohol was not the center of our relationship, you and I simply were not buddies. We did not hang out together unless we were drinking.

I finally hit the wall in June of 1983. I was at the tail end of a week-long binge, and it felt like the morning had lasted nearly as long as the twentieth century. My mouth tasted like the Russian Army had washed their socks in there, and I had to walk very slowly because I was afraid that I was going to break. I desperately needed a drink. I needed to stop somewhere and put my fire out with whatever brand of high octane liquid that was available. Any port in a storm.

It was nearly noontime and I was suffering from a world-class hangover. The only thing that mattered to me was getting a few Bloody Marys to pour down the hatch and lubricate all of my moving parts. I made my way to Boston's North End and into the European Restaurant because that happened to be the direction in which my nose was pointing at the time, certainly not because The European had a reputation for extremely great bloodies, which it most certainly did not.

I know that I looked for all the world like a respectable young man in a proper business suit stopping for lunch in one of Boston's trendier areas. No matter how much I suffered internally, I always found a way to make it look good on the outside, a skill that would prove to be very useful in the years to come. It was the early eighties and I looked the consummate Yuppie. To the casual observer I must have looked like just another of the many "suits" stopping to grab a quick bite to eat as I moved along from one part of a very busy day to another, the actual act of eating lunch having about as much meaning as the next phone call.

But this consummate yuppie didn't care a whit if he ever ate another thing for the rest of his life. There was a volcano boiling up inside, and if I didn't get a drink before too long, that volcano was going to erupt and it was going to get very ugly. This was at least a four-drink hangover, and I desperately needed to grab hold of a "hair of the dog that bit me." An eternity passed between the time I gave the waitress my drink order and the time she finally materialized with the magic tonic. Some people are so damned slow that the only gear they seem to possess is reverse. I swear to God, I was drooling, probably even foaming at the mouth, by the time she put that drink down in front of me. I grabbed hold of that glass with every ounce of life and determination I could muster. I

Chapter Two - Make A Commitment To Your Choice

can still picture that glass and feel it in my hand, 20 plus years later. The most amazing medicinal cure known to man is the wonderful curative power that ingesting any kind of alcohol has in eliminating the common hangover. Even a four-drink hangover like this one.

But the cure did not work. The medicine had finally failed.

I was seriously screwed.

Instead of rejuvenating me as they always had, instead of breathing enough new life into me to get me through the rest of the day, instead of serving as the starting point of the next inevitable drunk, these noontime drinks were going down like crushed glass. And I knew it was all over. Every microorganism of my body and being screamed at me, and I knew right down to the pit of my soul and beyond that I just could not do it anymore. Life as I knew it had just ended.

I surrendered.

But what to do?

Chapter Two - Make A Commitment To Your Choice

MEET THE TAG TEAM

Believe it or not, I was actually in therapy at the time and had been for a couple of years. Not with just one therapist, mind you. I seemed to need two of them. A veritable therapeutic tag team. Not only did I see them on an individual basis, but I also was involved in a group therapy setting under their supervision. Thank God I had the good sense to seek help at one time in my life, and, for a while anyway, they really helped me. Of course, given the condition I was in when I first met them, Sigmund Freud's dog could have been helpful to me.

So I did the only thing I could think to do and I called them to make an appointment for the following day, a Friday. During this meeting I made an agreement to stop drinking for 30 days in order to "stabilize" myself. There was never any mention of detox, Alcoholics Anonymous, or treatment of any sort. In fact, during a subsequent group therapy session (you'd think that with all this therapy going on, somebody would have caught on to me by now), my therapist made an emphatic point of telling the members of the group that I was not an alcoholic. This was ok with me because I simply didn't know any better. I just wanted the pain to go away, and I didn't care what I had to do to bring that about. I would have called myself an aardvark if that would have eased the pain just a fraction.

Truth be known, I never really gave much thought to what course of action or treatment might be best for me because, by the time I arrived at the point where I knew I had to stop drinking, I was quite incapable of much independent thought. I also didn't have the slightest idea what was wrong with me. I only instinctively knew that if I ever took another drink, it would eventually kill me. The only knowledge or experience I ever had with Alcoholics Anonymous was that my father wouldn't go, and everybody seemed to want him to. My father was in and out of detox almost as often as he put the key in the front door of our house. Therefore, going to detox or treatment was not an option that I was going to arrive at on my own. So I took the only course of action available to me at the time, and I followed the suggestion of abstention for 30 days. When the initial 30 day sentence had been served, I opted in for another 30 days.

I had no idea that by making a commitment to remain alcohol-free without a program of recovery I was literally sentencing myself to six and a half years of increasingly worsening mental anguish, emotional pain, and spiritual bankruptcy. I did not know that I had become an alcoholic, I did not know I had acquired a totally debilitating disease, and I did not know that I did not know. During those six-plus years, I was instructed by my erstwhile therapeutic tag team that I was not to pay any attention at all to things like thoughts or feelings. There was never a mention of alcohol. My job was to structure my day very tightly and to make sure that I did everything I planned to do. Therefore, I drove a schedule from 5:00 am to midnight and beyond, every day, running from one thing to another. And I became sicker and sicker without the slightest clue as to what could possibly be wrong with me.

It was only through an incredible string of seemingly unrelated coincidences, which I know today was the Hand of God moving me in the right direction, that I ended up as a member in good standing of Alcoholics Anonymous. Six and a half excruciating years and many broken relationships later, I finally discovered that I had a disease and that it was a life-threatening disease. I also found out the disease of alcoholism could never be cured. But it could be arrested, one day at a time.

Chapter Two - Make A Commitment To Your Choice

Once you have crossed over the invisible line from party animal to the actual disease of alcoholism, there is no turning back. A pickle can never again become a cucumber. You will always have the disease, and it is progressive. It is not unlike having cancer. Unless you take your daily medicine, it will grow and become stronger every day. The medicine for anyone suffering from the disease of alcoholism is The Twelve Steps Of Recovery and the fellowship of others who suffer from the same disease.

The reason I had become sicker and sicker over the six-plus years between putting down the drink and finally finding the fellowship of Alcoholics Anonymous is that my disease was progressing, untreated, while I tried to hold myself together with bubble gum and paper clips. I steadfastly denied myself the relief of a drink, which, at a very deep level, I knew would most assuredly lead to an untimely death. I also however, unwittingly denied myself the relief of the medicine to arrest my disease because I didn't even know I had a disease. So why would I ever try to find a cure for it? Also, and this is very important to anyone just starting out on a path of peace; I did not know that I did not know.

We will later discuss this phenomenon of not knowing that we don't know in significantly more detail, but for now suffice it to say we think and behave in ways we have learned right from the time we were innocent little babies are the ways we *should* think and behave. More often than not, we don't know that there is a more effective way for us to think and behave. We do not know that we could easily live our lives in a much more fulfilling and significantly more fun manner simply by making a different choice. And we don't know that we don't know. We seem to need someone or something to show us the way, and we need to trust whomever or whatever that is to take care of us along the way. For me, that someone or something is God, The Twelve Steps of Recovery, *A Course In Miracles,* and all the people I meet and whose books I read who are walking a spiritual path and who can shed some light on the path I am walking. I just need to be willing enough to listen, accept, and apply what seems to fit my particular situation, and leave all else aside.

For those of you reading this book who don't know much about alcoholism, the insanity of that disease of alcoholism is such that the one thing that could grant me at least a brief respite from the mental, emotional, and spiritual suffering I was enduring is the very same thing that would eventually have killed me. Had I picked up one drink during my dry-drunk phase, and I was tempted on many occasions because the oblivion of a blackout seemed far preferable to the agony of blind abstention, I am quite clear that I would never have been able to stop. Alcohol is significantly more powerful than my ability to control it. For someone like me, one drink is too many and a thousand aren't nearly enough. I am fairly clear that I would eventually have wrapped my car around a tree or a bridge abutment and I would not be here to write this book today. Fortunately, I was more afraid of drinking than I was of not drinking. Fear does have its advantages at times.

Somewhere near the end of the excruciatingly painful dry-drunk phase, a meeting was arranged by the erstwhile therapeutic tag team for the purposes of ending our relationship and going our separate ways. They couldn't wait to get rid of me. I had given much thought as to what I would say to them and I had read volumes of material in search of an answer as to exactly what was wrong with me. I didn't have a clue. They constructed this meeting in such a way as to place responsibility for what was wrong with me squarely on my shoulders,

Chapter Two - Make A Commitment To Your Choice

thereby taking the position that they had done the best they could for the poor misguided soul that I was. This was a little like Pontius Pilot washing his hands before condemning Christ to death.

During this meeting I had a rather unusual and profound experience. I told the tag team that, although I had looked at about a million different possibilities and had read about as much as I could possibly read, I still didn't have a clue as to what could possibly be wrong with me. And then some words came out of my mouth that had never before even remotely occurred to me. These words did not come from me because I was constitutionally incapable of devising such concepts. The words filled my being with a certainty that I had not known for many years. They came from the same place as the realization, one afternoon six-plus years earlier as I suffered at the European Restaurant in Boston's North End, that I could never drink again. These words did not come from me; they came through me, and I knew with absolute certainty that they were the only things I knew to be true.

I told the tag team that while I did not know what was wrong with me, I did know two things. I told them that I knew I had to get God into my life somewhere, somehow, some way, and I didn't know how to go about doing that. I also told them that I really needed to tell someone my story. I really did not have any idea what that meant, but I knew right down to the bottom of my soul that I desperately needed to tell someone my story.

Now, you'd think that after eight or nine years of therapy, I would have gotten around to telling them my story, or they would have found the skill enough to drag it out of me. I also truly believed that I did tell them all about me so I really did

81

not know what those words that came to me during our last meeting could possibly mean. But that is not how it all went, and as I now know, *everything happens for a reason.*

From where I sit today, many years later, it is absolutely no surprise to me that the two things I knew I needed in my life soon came to me in magnificent abundance.

Not long after my last meeting with the tag team, I found myself, through a string of coincidences that in itself is a rather fascinating tale, deeply immersed in the fellowship of Alcoholics Anonymous, joyfully telling my story to an understanding audience, and finding the God that I had sought for so long. I realized that the Grace of God was with me all along, steadily and invisibly moving such a brain dead-entity as I was in the right direction. I realized that God never left me because it is impossible for that to happen. I had simply separated myself from the awareness of the Grace of God and the Love of God in my life. I finally came to understand that I am no different than anyone else in the world. So if God is doing for me what I cannot do for myself, then He is doing it for everyone else as well. The trick is to consciously connect with that most amazing of powers. I began to build a foundation that gave me the strength to explore many different avenues of spiritual growth and development, a strength for which I am profoundly grateful today.

Chapter Two - Make A Commitment To Your Choice

LIFE AS A DRY DRUNK: IT ISN'T FUN

The time between the day I stopped drinking (June 8, 1983) and the day I crawled into my first AA meeting six and a half years later was quite difficult, to say the very least. Of course, I understand today that I needed to have that experience in order to learn the lessons that came with it so I could turn around and teach the lessons to someone else. But I did not know that then. In fact, I didn't know a whole lot other than what my therapists told me to do. I was instructed to plan my days very tightly and then execute the plan, which I did in spades. We began to focus on not what might be wrong with me internally, but on what I planned to do every day and how I executed the plan. We were intent on making me look good and virtually never talked about how I felt. It was like the old skit from Saturday Night Live where one of the characters liked to say, "No, no, Nando, you little schnook. It is not how you feel, it is how you look. And you look Marvelous!"

I was in sales at the time, and this gave me something to pour my enormous store of energy into, which certainly helped my business to grow and grow. I was exercising on a daily basis and doing a significant amount of volunteer work so I had plenty with which to occupy my time. As I made more money, I bought nicer cars and a number of properties, and I looked pretty good on the outside. I presented myself well while I was dying little by little on the inside.

I tried to live a normal life, to look cheerful all the time no matter what was going on with me, to make a difference in the non-profit agencies like the Big Brother Association in which I decided to invest some volunteer time, and to see what I could do about developing a loving relationship in my life. I lived from day to day, hoping with all my heart that when I woke up in the morning I would somehow magically begin to feel at home in my own skin.

This is the background story of what was happening in my life at the time I met my redheaded date for a drink at the Spinnaker restaurant. She appeared about half way through the dry-drunk phase and, as nuts as I was on the night I met her for a drink at the Hyatt, it was all downhill from there. I knew that I was out of my mind, I knew that I was full of emotions that I could not account for, which led to a life of constant confusion and frustration. I then ran these tumultuous feelings through the "universal-lousy-feeling-to-totally-misguided-conclusion" translator in my brain and decided that there must be something fundamentally flawed in my basic composition.

Perhaps I was missing some vital connecting parts and I was constitutionally incapable of having a normal interaction with anyone. I believe that if I had I been able to make this conclusion with absolute certainty, I probably would have felt at least some relief. At least I would have known that I was attempting to accomplish something of which I was biologically incapable, and that realization would surely have taken some of the pressure away. But nothing in my life was that simple, so I continued to work my ass off to make it look as though I was as normal as the day is long.

I didn't know what was wrong with me, I didn't know why ridiculous, crazy, nutso-gonzo, and insane thoughts were constantly rocketing through my head. I had no idea why I would then hold onto such insane thoughts with the ferocity of a hungry dog on a meaty bone. No matter how much I tried, I couldn't let go of them. I would then judge myself with the harshness of a Spanish Inquisitor for having such horrible

Chapter Two - Make A Commitment To Your Choice

thoughts. I berated myself because I believed that since I had such crazy thoughts going through my head, I must believe them. And what did that mean about me? This went on for years, one miserable day followed by yet another slightly more miserable day.

My redheaded friend (or was she a blond?) was fortunate in that she ran into me only about halfway through the dry-drunk phase, when I still had at least a smidgeon of humanity left that I could access. All I could think of when she and I were together was whether or not she was going to volunteer to pick up the very small tab. I knew this thinking was ridiculous and wrong, and I worked my ass of to get rid of it, but I just could not do so. What the hell was wrong with me? I had plenty of money; it wasn't about money. What was this all about and why could I not get rid of this insidiously minute and excruciatingly small thinking? The levels of lunacy to which my thinking was going to devolve by the end of the dry-drunk phase were entirely shocking compared to what was going through my head at the Spinnaker Restaurant.

More often than not, I felt like I was caving in on myself. My thinking was becoming more and more restricted and fundamentally different from that which I really believed at deeper levels. But I couldn't access that deeper thinking to save my life, and the more I struggled with it the worse it became for me.

I was latching onto crazy thoughts and reacting to them as though they were real all the time. My feelings would then line up accordingly, leading to a place where the range of thoughts I was capable of entertaining and the emotions that would course through me as a result of this narrow and generally negative thinking would create an enormously fast and irre-

85

versible downward spiral.

I would have a stray thought about something, realize that it was crazy, decide there was something wrong with me for having such a thought, search for the fundamental flaw inside me that could create such a terrible thought, feel an increasing sense of anguish when I could not identify the source, and panic when I realized that I could not get rid of the thought. This entire process oftentimes took place in a matter of seconds.

At the same time, there was another, much deeper part of me, a part of me that I was aware of and could not access, The Real Me, that completely understood I was only lying to myself. I would remember what it was like growing up as a very decent and cheerful child, and I just couldn't reconcile that with the crazy thinking and emotionally restricted adult I had obviously become. Then I would feel worse.

I was able to look back at myself as a fifth grader growing up in Boston and I would remember how much I loved to go to the library, on my own, and explore as many books as I possibly could. I would remember that for a long time my favorite movie was *Polyanna* because the main character was such a positive person and it resonated so fully with something similar inside me. I recalled how, as a very young child, I would actually quote lines from the movie to people who seemed to be stuck in a negative place because I understood that no matter how bad something seemed to be, there was always something positive to be found. All you had to do was find a way to change how you thought about it.

Every once in a while, fleeting images of happiness and contentment from my childhood would come back to me, and I

Chapter Two - Make A Commitment To Your Choice

wondered to where that kid had so completely disappeared. And why I was unable to bring him back for an encore appearance? I remembered how happy I was when my parents bought us a new house to live in, even if it did mean that we had to move to another neighborhood and I had to share a room with my four brothers. I remembered the love I felt for my newborn baby sisters even if I had no idea how to express that love. Five boys came first in my family, and finally getting a little baby sister was certainly something special. And I remembered how wonderful I felt whenever I went to visit my father in the firehouse and how good it made me feel to know that I was the son of a man who saved people's lives for a living.

Whenever I was having one of those episodes of really crazy, bizarre, and tenacious thinking I always had moments of remembering life as a relatively good kid. And I would wonder what happened to that kid, the one who shined his shoes to go out and hang on a street corner and try to look tough, the one who was actually voted as having the best disposition by the other kids in his eighth-grade class, the one who so much enjoyed doing things for other people just for the sake of doing them. I couldn't help but compare how divergent the jagged thinking of the present was from the warm and fuzzy thinking of the past - and then become even more terrified as to what the future was going to be like.

It is much easier to write about this time of my life in retrospect than it was to actually live through the experience, but live I did. Yes, I was thoroughly confused by the rocketing roller-coaster ride of conflicting emotions that relentlessly bombarded me every minute of every day. I didn't know why I was out of my mind all of the time, and I had no idea what was wrong with me. Perhaps a lobotomy would help. Surely, if someone had come along and shown me that a brain transplant would fix the problem, I would have signed on the dotted line in an instant. Yet throughout it all there remained something deep inside that just wouldn't go away, something I couldn't put a name or a face to, something that was beyond my understanding, a light that no matter how badly I felt or crazy and confused my thinking had become, I just could not extinguish. I believe that it was this light that kept me going when suicide was a very real option for me. This is the very same light that lives in everyone, the light that is our source of happiness and peace, the light that is everyone's birthright, the light that is the love of God.

I had not yet come to the realization that the purely innocent and totally loving child that first crawled out of my mother's womb didn't go anywhere; he had simply been buried under the rubble of what I learned to think was important. He had been efficiently pushed aside by erroneous ideas about how things *should* be. I had not yet learned that the child who took his first breath of air on a cold winter day in February of 1954 was, and always will be, an expression of the eternal love of God. I had not yet come to the understanding that only the love of God is real and that every person on the face of the earth is an equal expression of that love, whether they know it or not. And I certainly did not yet know that because the love of God is the actual source of everyone's existence, nothing could ever take that away from me because it is impossible to be separated from our source.

We are all as much a part of God as a drop of water is a part of the ocean, and there isn't anything anyone can do about that. One can certainly and quite successfully deny this reality either consciously or unconsciously, but there isn't one blessed thing that anyone can ever do to change it. And to the

Chapter Two - Make A Commitment To Your Choice

extent that we are able to come to accept this, we will enjoy true and lasting peace in all of our daily affairs. But this learning was to come slowly and much later. In the meantime, I had more suffering to endure.

Chapter Two - Make A Commitment To Your Choice

THE LESSON OF THE STORIES, THE STORY OF THE LESSONS

One of the things I have really grown to love is taking a step back and watching the events of my life unfold. I thoroughly enjoy noticing the connections and coincidences that lead one event into the next, according to a script that I could never come close to writing, no matter how much creative genius I might bring to the table. Someone once told me that coincidence is God's way of remaining anonymous. Sounds about right to me. There will be several stories of this nature in this book. I don't seem to be able to separate that which I would like to teach from the experiences I have had along the way. No matter how much a person reads and learns what is found between the covers of books, no matter how much formal education a person has, it is our actual experiences and the willingness to learn the lessons of those experiences that will inform our lives the most.

Also, *A Course In Miracles* tells us to "teach Love because that is what you are." In other words, if you really want to learn something for yourself, teach it to someone else. If you want to learn love, teach love. If you want to learn peace, teach peace. Therefore, by sharing the lessons of my life with you, I am creating a win-win-win situation. I have credibility in your eyes because I am speaking from personal experiences; you get to see where you can apply some of what I have learned to your life and how much things aren't always what they seem to be; and I get to take yet another look at my own life and learn the lessons at a more profound level. It doesn't get much better than that.

Many of the stories in this book have a number of common threads woven into the background that you might miss unless I point them out. The first, and perhaps the most important is that we do not have any control over anybody or anything else - ever, end of story. Period. This is a basic truth that can take a considerable amount of work to wrap your brain around - and even more work to place into everyday practical application. It is easy to say that you do not have control over anybody or anything else, but backing those words up with observable and verifiable behavior that shows you actually *believe* such an outrageous concept and accept that it really does apply to you and everybody else...well, this is something else entirely. The ego would have you believe, and do so in a cleverly convincing manner, that you really *do* have control, and it is everybody else that does not. The ego tells you that it is your right to keep everything pretty well under your thumb because it is the best thumb that exists. The ego also tells you that it is not ok for anyone else to exert anything even remotely resembling control, especially if the recipient of their wayward schemes happens to be - at least according to your perception - you.

You will see that the old saying "if you want to hear God laugh, make a plan" is absolutely true. Living in the background of all my stories is the fact that once you make a decision and commit to it, the universe will open wide and pour your desires onto you in ways that you couldn't hope to imagine. As my stories unfold, you will see that all you really have to do to bring about the joy and happiness that the plans you so meticulously make are designed to achieve is follow your nose. Remember, we are no different, you and I, and if something is true for me, then it is true for you. If I can look at my life and find an irrefutable connection between what would otherwise seem to be simple random events, then I know you can do the same. The question then needs to be asked: Who is the architect of all these events?

Chapter Two - Make A Commitment To Your Choice

Which brings us to the subject of trusting a power greater than yourself to bring about the transformations that you would like to make. You will notice how seemingly random events which, when viewed in the ever-so-limited context of the event itself, can seem to be just that - a random and unimportant something that is unconnected to anything else and just happened to have occurred. But if you follow the path of how one event then connects to another, apparently unrelated and totally random event, you'll see that nothing is random and that everything indeed does happen for a reason. All you have to do is stop long enough to take a look and you will see, *by your own experience*, that what I am saying is true.

You will also notice that the only reason anything is brought into your life is to fulfill your particular personal desires, to bring you the happiness you so richly deserve by serving as a vehicle to teach you the lessons you need to learn. You begin to see in real time how that which just occurred could not possibly have happened unless a particular something had not already occurred. Also - and you need to pay very close attention to this because it is of excruciating importance and can actually help you to feel better right away - *the event that is currently happening in your life that is causing you so much grief is one of those events that you will later look back on and understand that it needed to happen in order for you to be where you are today*. The shitstorm in your life today is the very same shitstorm you will be grateful for five years from now. Why wait? Be grateful now; it will make a huge difference. That which is currently happening is a necessary thread in the unfolding mystery of your life, and you can embrace the experience rather than seek to hide from it.

Remember, if it will be funny three months from now, it is funny now.

Upon closer examination, it is not difficult to become awestruck by the magnificent beauty of the intricate tapestry that has been woven for you by the heretofore seemingly unrelated threads of your life. You then become even more awestruck when you understand that you could not possibly have written the script and really did not have much to do with how the drama unfolded. If you are brave enough, you will notice how everything has happened exactly how it was supposed to happen in order to bring you to exactly where you are now. By logical extension, then, everything that has yet to happen will also be for your benefit so there is really nothing to worry about, nor is there any need to force false control in order to make things work out the way you think they should. You have, *by looking at your very own life and your very own experiences thus far*, collected enough irrefutable data to support the contention that all you need to do is let go, because how you think things *should* be is infinitesimally small compared to how they *can* be.

Chapter Two - Make A Commitment To Your Choice

ONE OF MANY MIRACLES

The story of how I finally arrived at me first meeting of Alcoholics Anonymous is one of those scripts I could never have written on my own, much less envisioned. Remember, right up to the time I had my last meeting with the tag team in November of 1989, I did not know that I was an alcoholic. It was not long thereafter, however, that I began to suspect that my dubious relation with alcohol could possibly be the source of my considerable internal difficulties.

In January of 1990, after having just barely survived a holiday season that was intermingled with fake smiles worn for the benefit of whomever I happened to be spending time with and thoughts of either suicide or drinking again, I finally wandered into my first AA meeting. It was nothing to write home about. The heavens did not open up and God's voice could not be heard by everyone present, booming through the galaxies to announce the arrival of yet another stray child returning to the nest. However, I left the meeting with pleasant and hopeful feelings, thinking that I had found something that would help me. What happened to me the following day changed my life forever, and it was another one of those things that I could never have predicted.

The air was crisp and cool with a bright blue sky and a slight breeze that gently kissed the rosy cheeks of everybody who was out and about on Boston's waterfront that day. It was the kind of day that felt a whole lot warmer than the thermometer told you it really was because there wasn't a cloud in the sky to interfere with the wonderful warming rays of a friendly January sun. I had parked my car and was walking toward my first noontime AA meeting, walking toward something that seemed to be calling me toward it, pulling me along like a pile of thin iron shavings irrevocably drawn to a nearby powerful magnet. I walked with a sense of certainty, knowing that I was doing something that was very good for me.

The meeting was at the Boston Coast Guard base, a facility built on inner harbor waterfront property that was the envy of every real estate developer who had ever been heard to utter the mantra, "location, location, location." This property would return millions to anyone who could convert it into the high-priced condominium units or luxury hotels that already lined the wharves to the south of the Coast Guard facility. Yet I can assure you that thoughts of real estate values or making millions on lucrative development deals never crept into my mind as I briskly walked toward that fateful meeting. I was much too preoccupied with thoughts of survival.

If you were orbiting the earth in a geosynchronous orbit and you just happened to be able to peer down and watch me as I entered that meeting, you couldn't help but notice that, on the surface, I was definitely in the wrong place. I was wearing a light tan-colored London Fog overcoat with a dark blue suit and a starched white button-down shirt. My shoes were highly polished and I wore a bright red power tie. I had learned much about dressing for success, which in my case translated into looking good on the outside even if I was crumbling like an abandoned sand castle on the inside.

Entering the room where the meeting was to be held was like walking through a portal and being deposited into another universe. The smoke was very thick, and everyone in there looked like society's worst preconceived notion of what an alcoholic looks like. Torn and ragged clothes were obviously the order of the day. Most of these people hadn't seen the business end of a hair brush or comb in half of forever, and all

Chapter Two - Make A Commitment To Your Choice

had the look of having just gotten released from about five years in the big house. People had huge railroad-track scars running across their faces, and many wore keys dangling from chains latched onto their belts. I certainly did not look like I belonged in that meeting.

And then an amazing thing happened.

I stopped to pour myself a cup of coffee, brave soul that I was, before trying to find a seat. All the while I couldn't help but think that everyone in the room was staring at me because I certainly stuck out like a sore thumb. The only thought that kept gushing through my head was along the lines of what the hell am I doing here? I found a seat with good and clear access to the door in case I needed to make a fast getaway. I promptly sat down, looked around, and said to myself; "My God, I'm home." And the feeling of having finally come home, the feeling of actually belonging somewhere, the absolute conviction that I was in the right place at the right time and that I was going to be well taken care of washed over me like the most refreshing and cleansing shower imaginable. I sat there with my jaw on my chest, stunned, unable to move or speak, and the thought "My God, I'm home" ran through my head, my heart, and my soul.

The really amazing part of all of this is that I had never, ever, used those words before in my entire life. Given the life I had led up to that point, I was totally incapable of such a sentiment. It was not me. They were not my words. Those words; "My God, I'm home" did not come from me and were the least expected words I could ever have muttered to myself. I had never felt at home, anywhere, in my entire life, and I had become so accustomed to feeling like an outsider that it was about as natural to me as breathing. So, to have the words

"My God, I'm home" suddenly appear out of nowhere was a spectacular event, especially considering that I was in a place where, on the outside at least, it would appear that I clearly did *not* belong. The words did not come from me; they couldn't have. And the reason that I sat there, stunned, with my jaw on my chest, was that I knew they came from God. I also knew that everything was going to be all right. It was the greatest sense of relief I have ever felt and one that I can still feel just writing about it today.

Little by little I began to recover because I began to take heaping portions of the medicine I needed to treat the life-threatening disease of alcoholism I had acquired, unbeknownst to me. Eventually, I discovered that the really good kid I once was, and whose fate I often wondered about, had really not gone anywhere. He was still alive and well, living deep down inside, patiently waiting for me to remember him. Every day I began to move a little bit closer, by conscious choice, to actually becoming the person that God originally intended for me to be. I did so by actively engaging in a process of removing all of the blocks that I had created to living a fully realized life. I was no longer so completely terrified that hiding was my only option. I had found hope.

Chapter Two - Make A Commitment To Your Choice

DECIDING HOW TO THINK

It occurred to me today as I walked down the stairs on the way to my home office for my morning session of writing that I like to use my life experiences as tools for teaching. The really important and complicated lessons are generally learned in hindsight. It is much easier to be a Monday-morning quarterback and call the right plays than it is to find effective modes of thinking and behavior while you are right in the middle of the game. It further occurred to me that if I looked at each experience in and of itself without trying to place it in the context of my whole life, I would really be missing the point. What I am trying to say and not doing a very good job of it is this;

If something is occurring in my life that is causing significant feelings to be aroused, no matter whether they are feelings of profound dread or unmitigated joy, I know that eventually I am going to look back at this particular experience and glean the lessons I need to learn as a result of having had the experience. I understand that hindsight generally shows me how the experience fits into the mosaic of my life as a whole, and I understand that whatever happened did so for a certain reason having only to do with me.

I have also become fairly clear that whatever happened is essentially given to me to facilitate my growth and learning, which is always good. Armed with this truth, I am then able to go through anything, anywhere, anytime, absolutely certain in the knowledge that I am right where I need to be and I am doing exactly what I need to be doing. I know, by looking at my own life up to this point, that everything will always turn out just fine, thank you very much, because it always has. Even if I do not think so right now, having been caught up in the middle of whatever happens to be going on, I will think so at some point in the future.

Therefore - and this is the good news - I can always take a step back *while the experience is occurring,* in real time, right in the middle of whatever shitstorm seems to be coming down on me, and decide that instead of waiting to learn whatever I need to learn in hindsight, I can look for the lessons while the storm is happening. This proactive approach is simply a process of making a decision to see things differently, which is precisely what *A Course In Miracles* describes as a miracle because it can transform your life and positively impact every person with whom you come in contact.

You can change the perception that life just dumped another load of crap all over you as well as the feelings that result from such a perception. You can transform such thinking into a deep and abiding understanding that you have just been given a wonderful opportunity to learn a valuable lesson. You can then be grateful for the experience because in the learning is the personal growth you very much desire. Changing your perception will always change your feelings. In other words, you always have the power to turn chicken shit into chicken salad. I have learned to look at the greatest challenges to come along and allow myself to feel the feelings of fear, panic, and dread that generally accompany such challenges because I know the only thing that is really occurring is I am on the high end of the learning curve. It helps.

And because you *always* have the power to choose your perception, you therefore *always* have the power to choose your feelings. As *A Course In Miracles* teaches, "I can see peace instead of this." I fully understand that exercising this option is not necessarily the easiest thing in the world to do. Doing so can often be rather terrifying in and of itself, which is cer-

Chapter Two - Make A Commitment To Your Choice

tainly enough to dissuade even the heartiest of souls. When this happens, all you really need to do is be willing to see things differently, be willing to see peace instead of this, be willing to have faith in a power greater than yourself, be willing to trust that God would never give you anything that was not specifically designed for your ultimate good, then sit back and watch the miracles pour forth.

And in those really difficult times, the times that you are convinced that nothing could ever work for you, those times you really know that there is no use going on because all the cards are really stacked against you, all you need is a little bit of willingness to see things differently. At those dark, bleak, and terrible times when you are sincerely convinced that no power on earth could or would do anything remotely in your favor, all you really need is the willingness to be willing. Muster up the energy to try a little willingness and you will eventually be amazed at the direction your life takes.

Willingness to do creates the ability to do.

It also means that we can constantly seek to stretch ourselves, allow ourselves to do the things that we never thought we could or should, to actively look for all kinds of new and exciting adventures, because we know that there is no such thing as a real risk. We conquer fear by acquiring the faith that all will be well, no matter what, because our hindsight has taught us everything that has already transpired in our lives is exactly what has been necessary. It has brought us to precisely where we need to be.

Opportunity and possibility are all that really exist.

Often we cannot know why something is happening to us,

which is understandable because we do not have the Big Picture, the perspective of God. This is one of the things that makes it all so much fun; you don't need to know. The point is that in hindsight we can connect the dots more easily than we can now. Yet, in the now, it is extraordinarily easy to get caught up in feelings of fear, trepidation, terror, guilt, remorse, and self-doubt because they are the defaults we have so dutifully built up over time. It is too easy to lose the perspective that what is happening today is merely another blip on the screen. If you maintain that perspective, though, fear of the future becomes unnecessary because the future is guaranteed.

For me, I needed to have everything that happened in my life - from slamming my car into a tree that would not budge at the age of 19, to becoming alcoholic and not knowing, from putting down the drink in a spiritually inspired moment at the European, to living through six and a half years of progressive hell as a dry drunk, from meeting and leaving the erstwhile therapeutic tag team, to the soul-searing awakening at my second AA meeting - in order to put me into the mental, emotional, and spiritual state of readiness that was absolutely necessary for the foundation upon which to make the biggest commitment of my life.

You may be thinking right now that the commitment this chapter is all about was, for me, the commitment I made to stop drinking. Not even close. As big as that particular commitment was, it pales in comparison the one I made later, the one this chapter is about. I am talking about the Big Kahuna, the mother lode of commitments, the commitment that, once made, guaranteed I would eventually enjoy the sense of peace, serenity, and joy that exists in my life today. These feelings will always exist for me unless I decide to change my

Chapter Two - Make A Commitment To Your Choice

mind, which I can't see happening at any time in either the near or far off future.

But before I tell you about The Big Commitment, there is another story that needs to be told.

Chapter Two - Make A Commitment To Your Choice

HOW I MET MY WIFE: ANOTHER MIRACLE

Once upon a time - and it seems like a very long time ago, although it *feels* like just yesterday - I was graduated from Boston Technical High School. I can't tell you why, but my ambition at the time, as reported in the caption below my picture in the school yearbook, was to hitchhike to California. If you stay with the story long enough, I will show you how including that ambition in my yearbook ultimately led me to marriage and children, a plan that I never could have devised in my wildest and most creative imagination. I will also show you how everything always works out exactly the way it should for you, and all that you need to do is let go, get yourself out of the way, and allow your fondest dreams to be handed to you on a silver platter. You are not in charge.

David Spillane was one of the guys in my high-school graduating class but I did not know him at all while going to school. I met him through Walter Duscza, who was also a member my graduating class. I knew Walter because he and I worked for the same company delivering packages in downtown Boston after school. Finding that job for me was the only good thing that my "guidance" department was ever able to pull off, being as overworked, underfunded, and lethargic as the department was. At any rate, Walter introduced me to David, and the three of us became fast friends.

One day David just happened to be looking through the yearbook. He noticed that my ambition was to hitchhike to California and asked me if I really wanted to go for it. I did. But when it came time to put the rubber to the road I didn't have enough money so David bought a car and took his younger brother. Before going, however, David actually gave me his job in the mail room of a company called Carter Rice, which was a wholesaler of paper to the printing and publishing industries. David saw the mail room job was much better than the warehouse job I had at the time, realized it would be a step up, and put the deal together without any prodding from me. It was his idea. I had nothing to do with it. I would be able to work part time in the afternoons while I attended classes at U/Mass Boston in the morning. Such a deal!

I actually ended up taking a leave of absence from school and quitting my job at Carter Rice a couple of years later to jump in a van and take off on a cross-country adventure with three other friends. The mystique of a laid-back life style, long hair, sex, drugs, and rock and roll was just too alluring to let pass by while I was still young and irresponsible enough to make such a decision. I would also still have enough time left to recover from the fallout should there be any. This was the fall of 1973. The war in Vietnam was still raging, American kids were getting killed by the bucket load, and I had just narrowly escaped getting drafted. However, the dream of living a life of sun and surf in the anything-goes fantasy of Southern California turned into the reality of not being able to find adequate work and eventually running out of money. I ended up having my parents wire me the money to fly home. How embarrassing is that? Well, I went back to work at Carter Rice, resumed my education at U/Mass, and moved back into my parents' house, having enjoyed many outrageous misadventures and learning some significant lessons as a result of making the decision to take off and hit the road.

I worked my way up to a position in outside sales after I graduated from U/Mass and began to make more money than I ever thought possible. I also had a great expense account and thought it was mighty terrific of the company to be the prime sponsor of my increasingly unquenchable thirst. The business

Chapter Two - Make A Commitment To Your Choice

was rather simple, yet the human propensity to complicate the living shit out of anything never ceased to amaze me. We bought paper from various paper mills and resold it to printing and publishing companies. Easy cheesy. My job was very simply to sell a product to people who *had* to buy it from somebody. I just needed to make sure that the somebody was me. Not a bad gig at the time.

Jack Bushman was the Northeastern Regional Sales Manager for Hammermill Paper Company, and it was his job to manage the relationship between my company and his mill, a relationship that was a fairly intimate one in that Hammermill owned Carter Rice. Jack showed up in our office on the same day every week (I believe it was on Wednesday), always armed with an off-color joke and a good heart. At some point Jack passed my name along to Dave Lionet, a man who sold insurance for Northwestern Mutual. Dave was rather adept at asking satisfied customers like Jack Bushman if he knew of anyone beginning to make their way in the world that Dave could contact to discuss life insurance. Jack gave Dave my name, and Dave contacted me.

I was single at the time, having drunk myself out of my first marriage without ever knowing it. Of course, the case could also be made that I drank myself *into* the marriage to begin with, so it was really quite a blessing that we were only married for nine months. I eventually met with Dave and ended up buying a large whole-life policy from him, which I know delighted him. By this time, I had stopped drinking and I was already steadily marching toward the penultimate level of spiritual and emotional bankruptcy imaginable.

Dave and I were able to develop a fairly good working relationship because by then I had become talented at making it

107

look good on the outside while on the inside I slipped inexorably toward a very deep and miserably dark abyss. Also, I was good at developing working relationships with people because I only had to interact with the other person on a very limited basis. That didn't give me enough time to get in my own way and blow the thing to kingdom come, which is what I always did if anyone got too close to me.

Knowing that I was single and that I was enjoying more and more success in business, and having experienced the somewhat pleasant individual that I am capable of being at times (back then I had to work at being pleasant, whereas nowadays it is simply a natural extension of who I really am), Dave one day suggested that I look into a certain singles organization that he had once joined and that he very much enjoyed. He mentioned that there were many women members who found themselves in circumstances similar to my own and that I would most likely be able to meet someone as a member of the Post Club, just like he had done.

Well, I did not bite at this suggestion because I had my own foolproof methods of meeting women and insuring that I had plenty of female companionship. First, I made the irrevocable decision that I would not date anyone who worked for the same company I worked for. Next, I extended that decision to include any women who worked in any aspect of the graphic arts industry because the business was just too small, thank you very much, and sooner or later everyone would be privy to my most private and embarrassing affairs. I also didn't think it would be a very good idea to date anyone who was in any way connected to the many non-profit and social service agencies to which I donated a significant amount of volunteer time. On the whole, I had actually developed a very effective strategy of keeping myself completely out of intimate relation-

Chapter Two - Make A Commitment To Your Choice

ships for quite a while, duly placating my extreme terror of closeness and intimacy.

In retrospect I can plainly see that my thinking and scheduling activities helped make it impossible to meet someone in whom I could develop a romantic interest, although, at the time I would have told you that I was actively looking to develop a relationship with someone, because I really thought I was. My propensity for planning my time right down to the minute actually sealed my fate by making it particularly difficult to find the time for intimacy and romance. I did not understand that I had developed a very effective strategy of hiding in plain sight while I allowed fear to run my life. The policy worked for me in that I was more afraid of intimacy than I was of solitude. Besides, I didn't have time to get lonely. I was under orders from the erstwhile therapeutic tag team to plan my day and execute the plan.

It is exceedingly easy to perpetrate all manner of lies on oneself if those lies firmly support the ego's goals of smallness and restriction.

The ego will always keep you from becoming the person you really are and from doing that which more fully enhances your life and the lives of those with whom you come in contact. The goal of the ego is smallness, restriction, and death, while you are actually wired for love, freedom, peace, and greatness.

But Dave Lionet was a salesman's salesman, as professional as the day is long, and he firmly believed in exchanging leads with other understanding sales professionals in order to expand his business. Every meeting or telephone conversation I ever had with Dave invariably ended with him asking me who I could recommend him to contact. And so it was that when I received a couple of messages on my telephone answering machine from Monique at the Post Club, I knew exactly how she had gotten my name. But I also deleted the messages with the speed of a Michael Jordan drive to the hoop. Fear will always rule with an iron hand whenever fear is allowed to rule. However, the existence of the Post Club became neatly tucked away in the file drawer of my mind marked "for future reference," and I went on with what would pass on the surface as a reasonably balanced life. Another fear-induced illusion. Also, how contrived does the name "Monique" at the Post Club sound, and what was Lionet really trying to get me involved in anyway?

As I look back on that time in my life, it is clear to me (and it may already be clear to you) that I wasn't only hiding from intimate relationships, I was hiding from *any* relationship. I was also hiding from myself.

Chapter Two - Make A Commitment To Your Choice

YOU JUST NEVER KNOW

I grew up in Dorchester, Massachusetts, which, at the time of my childhood was the Irish/Catholic bastion of blue collar, working-class, Democratic voting and above average-sized families. It was a part of The City of Boston that was dominated by three-decker houses that were built on postage stamp-sized lots and where family privacy simply did not exist. The Catholic Church was so dominant in Dorchester that every kid identified with the parish in which he lived. From the first to the fifth grade, I lived in St. Peter's Parish. My family moved to St. Kevin's, where I completed my grammar school education from grades six to eight while remaining under the stern tutelage of the Sisters of Charity of Halifax.

In every neighborhood of Dorchester there lived boat loads of kids. It was the duty of all Irish/Catholics to abstain from the practice of birth control. But abstention from the activities that would ultimately create the next mouth to feed was never an option. The old joke is quite correct: What do you call people who use the "rhythm" method of birth control? Parents.

There were so many kids on my street (and my street was really small by comparison) that we had enough boys around the same age to have our own football team. There were always people around. Especially in the summer when all three families that lived in a three decker would gather on the front porch during the evenings for conversation, conviviality, and copious amounts of beer.

I am one of seven children, third born, with more first cousins than I could possibly count. I was involved in many activities in which most of the kids my age participated and which were run by adults, one of whom was my father, so there was virtually never a time when I was not part of a larger crowd. Maybe that is why I so much loved to go to the library alone and spend many comfortable hours perusing the endless variety of escapes. I was always the quiet one in the crowd, never had much of an inclination to draw attention to myself. I didn't see the point. I had learned to develop an amazing talent of seeming to disappear in the middle of a fairly large group of people where everyone knew each other relatively well.

I learned to disappear because I was afraid. Why should I show anybody the talent that I really had or exhibit the intellect that was always there smoldering under some very tentative skin? Why would I ever take the risk associated with being my true self and standing out in the crowd, just to end up becoming the target of whatever cruel ridicule children are most capable. Better to hide and get by. Better to give in to the developing fear, provide it a fertile plot of ground from which to take nourishment, and helplessly sit back while it slowly grew into an overpowering force of nature. Hiding my true self, the real me, from myself and others, became a way of life for me. It was a process that would not begin to be reversed until the day I found the Twelve Steps which ultimately led me to a study of *A Course In Miracles* and the awakening that I so desperately needed and desired.

One day - and I can't remember if there were any extenuating circumstances that prompted me to not only think about it but to take action as well - I decided that it was time to meet some women and have a little bit of dating fun. I had enough recovery under my belt, I was on a fairly solid footing in my relationship with God, and I was ready. When you are ready and willing to make a change, the change will occur. This is another way of saying that when the student is ready, the teacher will appear. So I reached back into the deep recesses

Chapter Two - Make A Commitment To Your Choice

of my somewhat faulty memory and Dave Lionet's recommendation of The Post Club came slamming front and center. There was nothing else to do but call and join. I actually ended up meeting Monique at The Post Club and was rather surprised to find that she was a real person and that Monique was really her name. Needless to say, I started meeting some wonderful women and I had an absolute blast.

I must say that the people at The Post Club, and Judith Shea in particular, really went out of their way to make what could otherwise be a frightful and stressful experience a rather pleasant one instead. The way the process worked was that you had to do an extensive interview with a staff member to make sure you fit the membership profile. A little bit of exclusivity and snobbery here. The intake process served the dual purpose of having the particular staff member get a fairly good idea of who you are and the type of person you were looking to meet. He or she would then try to sell you a membership, which in my case was not very challenging because I had already decided to purchase a membership when I made the initial phone call. Judith was my Post Club representative and she became a mentor of sorts, walking me through the process, and doing a little bit of match-making on the side.

After becoming a member, the first order of business was to make an appointment with a professional photographer and have some shots taken. These photographs were then placed in a book with a personal profile I had to complete. The photos and the profile lived on facing pages so that each member had their own spread in the book. All the books were kept in the club's library for easy access by everyone. Next, I had to do an interview on video tape. The theory, which worked rather well in practice, was that I could go into the library any time I wanted and peruse the books containing the photos and written profiles of all the female members. If I saw someone that interested me, I would then go to the video viewing area and take a look at her actually speaking to another person. If I was still interested, I would let the person at the front desk (quite possibly Monique) know, and they would then send a postcard to the woman in whom I expressed an interest telling her that there was someone who would like to meet her. She could then come in to the club, check my photo and profile in the library, look at my video, and decide if she was interested as well.

Did I mention that I had a blast?

About a month and a half after I joined, Dave Knauer, one of my vendors, asked me if I wanted to play a round of golf with him at Stow Acres Country Club, a public golf course in the town of Stow where I lived. The golf course has a great reputation, but I never really got around to playing there because I was always too busy. Of course, the possibility also exists that I did not get around to playing much golf because I was such a lousy golfer and being too busy was a convenient excuse. Similarly, being too busy to meet women was really just a euphemism for abject terror. I later learned that being really "busy" was a great way to hide from myself.

Yet I also knew that I was a better golfer than Dave Knauer, so I gave it a little bit of thought and decided to take what turned out to be a beautifully sunny Wednesday morning at the end of June and play golf at Stow Acres. We hit many shots, had a lot of laughs, and we finished up at around noon time. There I was, looking at an afternoon off with nothing planned, which was very uncharacteristic of me. So I decided to go home, take a shower, and run into The Post Club to have a look around.

Chapter Two - Make A Commitment To Your Choice

It was always exciting to sit and look through the books of female members and know that if I came across someone I thought to be attractive, I could look at her videotape and get a little better impression of the actual person. If I was still interested, I could ask to have her look at my video. The chances were pretty good that I would eventually at least have an opportunity to meet her for a cup of coffee and then...well, you just never know. I was in a great mood when I walked in that day, and I was thoroughly enjoying myself as I perused the books of photos and bios, wondering what it would be like to meet certain women. I was fairly engrossed in what I was doing when my concentration was interrupted by a somewhat gravelly but nonetheless sweet voice saying hello to me. Elaine, who just happened to be in there that day as well, noticed me from across the room and - thank you God - decided to come over and sit down at the table where I was going through the books to say hello.

Needless to say, I was very interested and we ended up talking for quite some time. Eventually I excused myself to go and take a look at some videos. However, the only one I was really interested in looking at was Elaine's. So I walked into the video viewing room, selected her particular tape, and sat down to take a look. But I did not want her to see me looking so I kept my finger on the stop button of the video player in case she came in and walked by as I was watching. I was afraid that I would either die of embarrassment or that she would think I was just too weird to consider going out with.

Sure enough, I looked up after just a couple of minutes and there she was, walking toward me with a smile as wide, as bright, and as deep as I had ever seen. I immediately shifted to plan B and with my heart slamming into my throat and nearly choking off my air passages, I depressed the stop but-

115

ton for all I was worth. And the damn thing didn't work! I pressed it again, and it still didn't work! She walked by while I was actually watching her video so I rather adeptly shifted to plan C and promptly died of embarrassment.

That was June 26, 1991. We had our first official date on July 15, 1991 and were married one year and one month later on August 15, 1992. Thank you, God. But getting there was not the easiest thing in the world for me to do.

Chapter Two - Make A Commitment To Your Choice

THE COMMITMENT

Early on in our relationship, it was becoming clear to me that I really wanted to spend time with Elaine. I constantly felt the excitement and wonder of a naive teenager setting out on his very first dating adventure. Our second date was a round of golf on one of the hottest days of the year, but I didn't care. I had just gone out and purchased a new golf shirt and a new pair of shorts, so that I could at least look like I knew what I was doing. Also, it was extremely important to me to present myself properly. That I actually spent time shopping for just the right pair of shorts and just the right shirt to wear should have given me a clue that I was a goner. I never "shopped" for anything. Still don't. I like to go into a clothing store and walk up to the racks with my size on them, pick out the colors I like, and pay for them right away so I can get out as soon as possible. It was fun to be a teenager again.

Yet the fear that I always experienced whenever I began to get close to another person, or when they wanted to get close to me, constantly reared its ugly head. But I really did not know at the time that it was fear I was dealing with. Frankly, I didn't know *what* was wrong with me. Elaine and I would be moving along with all things going fairly smoothly and all of a sudden I would begin to feel a massive tension inside, a jagged kind of restlessness and horrible feeling that I just did not understand. Shortly thereafter, I would find myself picking a fight with Elaine and then trying, with every trick I could muster, to blame the whole thing on her. This was my modus operandi for many years before we met, and the habit had become fairly ingrained. In hindsight I understand that I was trying to push her away.

One day, I was sitting in the kitchen of our house in Stow (by this time we were living together and actively planning on getting married), and I felt an earthquake roiling inside. This was going to be the big one. I just wanted to crawl out of my own skin and create such a massive conflagration with Elaine that she would either immediately move out and promise never to see me again, or she would graciously poison my coffee. Whichever one happened didn't really matter to me. I could actually feel myself vibrating. The volcano that buried Pompeii was but an inconsequential hiccup compared to the eruption that was about to swallow the entire Eastern seaboard of the United States. I was ready, and I was not going to be denied.

And then another miracle happened.

For a reason that will forever remain a mystery to me, I stopped myself from creating the cataclysm that most assuredly would have put a very ugly end to our relationship. From out of the depths of my being came the realization that the only problem I had was fear. I had never previously considered that I was scared. I did not know that abject terror was the force that ruled my life. I had become so accomplished at looking good and acting like a "normal" human being that I do believe I began to buy my own bullshit and thought that I was actually ok. Yet I had a very difficult time creating intimate (or even close) relationships because I always got around to blowing them out of the water as soon as I inevitably became uncomfortable. Of course, my finger was always pointed at the other person as the cause of the problem. Why not? It was much easier than looking at me.

And here I was yet again, sitting in my kitchen, literally vibrating, getting ready to reduce yet another promising relationship to the ashes of oblivion when, all of a sudden, another voice was scratching at the door and begging to be let in.

Chapter Two - Make A Commitment To Your Choice

(Author's aside; I actually just figured out for the first time that the feeling, or realization if you will, that fear was the thing that was getting in the way came from the same place as the words "My God, I'm Home" came from at my second AA meeting. I might never have figured that out had I not decided to write this book. Yes!) For reasons that I, as yet, do not understand, I actually listened to this inner voice. I paid sufficient attention and gave it at least enough of a benefit of the doubt as to delay the inevitable eruption.

Instead, I turned and looked at Elaine, and I solemnly promised her that I would not let my fear get in the way. *I told her that no matter what, I would not allow my fear to get in the way of our relationship*. I refused to go there. No matter what. Plain and simple. This was the most solemn and heartfelt commitment I ever made, and I was determined to carry it through or die trying. There was nothing more important to me. I was committed. I did not know exactly what would happen as a result of making such a bold and, as I would eventually discover, all-encompassing commitment. It didn't matter. All I knew was that from that moment forward I refused to give in to the limitations that fear had always placed on my life. I would first root out the fear and then kick it right out the goddamn door.

There is a world of difference between making a commitment to doing something and being interested in doing it. If I am merely "interested" in doing something, I create a proverbial exit strategy for myself which gives me the option to get out if the going gets a little too rough. It also means that I am not really holding myself to any central standard because the standard can constantly shift around with the vagaries of my circumstances. Also, being merely interested gives me a way to take it easy on myself, to look like I am doing something when I am really only paying lip service to the issue at hand. Making a commitment has no exits. Being interested in doing something lacks the finality of commitment. The difference between being interested and being committed is like the difference between the ham and the eggs you have for breakfast; the hen is merely interested, while the pig is committed. Committed is the invading army that burns its boats on the beach. They have decided that they will win the fight or die trying. There is no third alternative.

This entire chapter was written to give you enough of a background on my life so that I could illustrate for you the depths to which I had emotionally, spiritually, and mentally plunged. You needed to have that information in order to accurately understand how monumentally huge making a commitment to eliminate fear in my life really was for me. In some ways I felt like I was going to die, but at the same time I never felt more alive. I can tell you that the act of making the commitment itself scared the living daylights out of me because I knew there was no turning back, and I had no idea what manner of demons were going to rear up and take a big bite out of my ass. Nor did I care. I had had enough of living a life filled with the limitations and restrictions dictated by fear, and now I was committed to a path with absolutely no downside. That's right - there is no downside to eliminating fear. Not a bad commitment to make.

I have learned so much as a result of making my commitment to eliminate fear that it may be somewhat difficult to impart how quintessentially magnificent a process it is in so many ways. But forget about the elimination of fear part for the moment. For the purposes of this chapter, I really only want to focus on the making of a commitment and what it really means.

Chapter Two - Make A Commitment To Your Choice

Rest assured that once you make a heartfelt (is there any other kind?) commitment to anything, your life will change. It will change immediately. This is a very good thing, for why else would one make a commitment in the first place if not for the fact that there existed a profound perceived need for a change to take place. This is one of the beautiful things about making a commitment to anything. If you ever find yourself standing at a crossroads, you must understand that everything that has previously happened in your life has occurred precisely in order to bring you to that point. You must choose your path and make a commitment to that choice. Once having done so, there is no going back to stand at the same crossroads because it is gone. A new circumstance has been added to your life now and nothing can ever be the same again. Of course, you could decide not to choose, which in itself is a choice. However, in not choosing and committing, you would be relegating yourself to a life of mediocrity, ruled by the same fear that prompted you to refrain from making a choice or a decision in the first place. You would be at the mercy of the meandering breezes created by those who have chosen, and you would be living a life of what Henry David Thoreau described as one of "quiet desperation."

However, once you make a commitment to something, once you stand at the crossroads and courageously choose your path, no matter what that path is, your whole world will change and the universe will open up and give you exactly what you need. You really do not have to do anything beyond making the commitment and pointing your nose in a new direction. Make your commitment, live your commitment in each moment of every day, to the best of your human ability, and God will absolutely take care of the rest.

God has the big picture. You and I only have the relatively

minute picture that our prior experience and fertile imaginations can provide. This is infinitesimal compared to the vision of God. Make your commitment to peace, or whatever you wish to commit to, and trust that God will bring you to places and provide you with experiences that you can't possibly imagine today. I know this to be true because it has been my experience, and there is no difference between you and me.

Allow me to give you an excellent example of how it works.

As soon as I told Elaine that I would not allow my fear to get in the way, she responded that she once read a book that might help me in this regard. *Love Is Letting Go Of Fear* was written by Gerald Jampolski, and it certainly sounded like exactly what I needed. It turned out to be much more.

Jampolski wrote the book after having discovered *A Course In Miracles,* and in it he put forth some of the more simple, yet nonetheless profound, principles embodied in *The Course.* It can really serve as a primer on *The Course*, and is rather easy to understand. But I was in such a state of mental and emotional disrepair that I had a very difficult time understanding anything he wrote. Every morning I would sit at the kitchen table studying the next couple of pages because that was all I could manage to try and understand. As a tool to help foster at least some remedial level of grasping this new-to-me material, I wrote the most important points out on index cards. I would then refer to the cards throughout the day because I knew there was something there for me, and I desperately wanted to find it. Focus and repetition might just work for me, I thought. I still have that book and those cards today.

But the amount of time and effort I put into studying *Love Is Letting Go Of Fear* is not the main point I wish to make here.

Chapter Two - Make A Commitment To Your Choice

What actually happened is that once I made a commitment, Elaine mentioned a book that ended up having a profound impact on me. This was not just any book, mind you, but just the *right* book for my particular circumstance and for what I had just committed to. A book that I never would have found had I not made the commitment to begin with. Significantly beyond the importance of the lessons I learned from *Love Is Letting Go Of Fear,* is the fact that the book also introduced me to *A Course In Miracles,* which exactly fit with the commitment to eliminate fear that I made, and then with the commitment I made to peace later in my life.

How profound is that?

I do not have be a rocket scientist to know with every fiber of my being that I am on the right path! I am being shown, in living color, every day.

Had I not been introduced to *A Course In Miracles,* I would not be writing this book today. If you are reading these words, you have benefitted (I hope) from the commitment I made many years ago. Had I merely decided to "work on myself" rather than make a specific commitment to the elimination of fear, the results would have been radically different. For one thing, I sincerely doubt that you would be reading these words because I can't imagine how I could otherwise have written the book. Further, if any of the choices and decisions you make as a result of having read this book have an impact on your life, either positive or negative, then every interaction you have for the rest of your life will, in some small way, be influenced by your having read this book. Therefore, the commitment I made many years ago will touch the people you have yet to meet. How cool is that?

I could not have written a script like this in my wildest dreams, and I could never have predicted that I would be sitting here writing this book. Hell, I could never have predicted that I would be living in the town I am living in, which is another story...

The point is that all you really need to do is make a commitment and then follow your nose. I promise that God will take care of the details. I urge you to make a commitment to peace. Seek to eliminate all thoughts and behaviors that are, in any way large or small, blocks to the experience of peace in your life. I am not asking you to run out and march down Main Street holding a sign proclaiming your commitment to living a life of peace. That is entirely unnecessary. All you need to do is refuse to entertain thoughts that are not peaceful and deliberately behave in ways designed to increase the experience of peace in your heart.

You will be amazed at how powerful you feel. I can assure you that the world you see will change in ways you couldn't possibly have predicted. How could I have predicted that including my ambition to hitchhike to California in my high school yearbook would ultimately lead to studying *A Course In Miracles* and writing this book? You will find yourself doing and saying things that you previously thought impossible. And you will simply scratch your head and smile, quietly floored by the unpredictability of it all, and thoroughly grateful for having made your choice for peace.

Making a commitment to eliminating fear in my life does not mean that, all of a sudden, fear was forever banished from rearing its ugly head. It does not mean that from that moment to the present day I have not experienced one moment of fear or one second of abject terror. I did not rub the dust off an

Chapter Two - Make A Commitment To Your Choice

antique lantern only to have a genie appear and wave a magic wand, granting my fervent wish to be forever fear-free. All it means is that I became hyper-vigilant. I began actively looking for the fear. I developed a habit of searching for those instances in my life where I was acting or thinking out of fear and made a decision to change the basis of the thought or action. I became highly sensitive to the forms with which fear manifested itself in my life and went about the work of eliminating the underlying fear so that the forms would also be erased. In some ways it was rather easy at the beginning because it was a pretty sure bet that any thought I had, or action I took, had some element of fear attached. It is like the old joke; How do you know when a lawyer is lying? His lips move. How do you know when George is experiencing fear? He is breathing.

Do I experience fear today? Yes. However, most of my fear, as well as the resultant anger and rage that are the favorite offspring of fear, is gone. I am, after all, a human being living in a world of duality. One of the key differences is that today I know that God will take care of the details. I trust Him in the same way I trust that in order for me to remain living, I need to keep breathing. All I have to do then is the next right thing. Trusting God will eliminate 90 percent of the fear that anyone could experience. The other 10 percent is for our own entertainment and learning pleasure.

Similarly, making a commitment to peace does not mean that from that moment forward my entire existence has been nothing but peaceful. Not at all. It does mean, however, that I remain in a state of heightened vigilance for those instances where I am experiencing unsettling thoughts, or where what I am doing is not conducive to maintaining or enhancing inner peace. My commitment is first to notice - and then to become willing to change whatever it is about my thoughts and actions that contributes to the turmoil I am experiencing. Interestingly enough, every time I notice a line of thinking or a course of action that is not peaceful, I also notice that fear is at the core of the problem. So, I get a two-for-one opportunity for change.

Remember, there is no downside in making a commitment to peace. It will cost you nothing. And it will reveal to you a clearly defined path, complete with unmistakable direction indicators and all the refreshments you need for the journey. Committing to peace will irrevocably lead you to your True Self.

You don't need to walk the path that I have walked to find real and lasting peace in your life. There are as many different paths available as there are people on the planet. You do not have to endure the pain that I endured. You have your own brand of pain, which is just as real to you as mine was to me. You do not have to become an alcoholic to learn the lessons of spiritual growth and development that I have learned along the way. This is not a story of suffering; it is a celebration of the life and love that is everyone's birthright. However, I do know that everything happens for a reason, and perhaps the reason I have gone through all the experiences I have in my life is to be able to put a more universal spin on them and turn them into lessons that can be helpful to you.

Besides, every single problem you have ever encountered, every difficult circumstance that has ever been presented to you, and every seemingly insurmountable obstacle that has ever been placed in your path, are merely variations on a theme. It is simply the same thing rearing up and appearing to you in a slightly different disguise. The culprit is fear. Plain

Chapter Two - Make A Commitment To Your Choice

and simple.

So the particulars of my experiences, the seeming magnitude of change that has taken place in my life over the past 20 years, or any of the lessons that can be gleaned from the aforementioned may appear to you, at a first examination, to have no relevance to your life, and you may be tempted to pack it up and move along. You would be making a big mistake.

Because the fear that caused me to drink the way I did is the same fear that causes someone else to run from relationship to relationship, always with the finger of fault pointing in the other person's direction. The fear that kept me from being able to develop any kind of relationship with a woman for such a long time is the same fear that blocks another person from enjoying peaceful relationships with family members or fellow workers. And the fear that caused me to react with anger every time I felt even remotely criticized is the same fear that drives all the anger anyone ever experiences. Fear is fear. Fear is the culprit. And it is only fear that can keep you from committing to and experiencing a life of peace.

Also - and I might as well go here while I am on a roll - every single entity or organism in the entire universe operates according to the exact same principles. The forces that sort and organize our universe, as well as all the universes beyond our universe, are the exact same forces that sort and organize every single cell in your body. It is all the same. As well, the dynamics that govern the relationships between individuals are the exact same dynamics that govern the relationships between countries, races, and religions. The dynamics in every single corporate entity on the face of the planet, no matter how large the company is or how many borders it crosses, are the same dynamics that govern every single family, government institution, political organization, non-profit agency, church group, religious hierarchy, or intimate relationship. It is all the same.

This is to say that the fear that fuels the fires of war and conflagration between nations is the exact same fear that is the foundation of racial prejudice throughout the world. The fear that causes a man to physically abuse his wife or children is the exact same fear that drives a woman to abandon a newborn infant, and the breath-stopping fear that leads to those terrible feelings of financial insecurity is the exact same fear that leads anybody to think that they are less than or not as good as someone else.

A Course In Miracles teaches us that we are either acting out of love or out of fear. These are the only two options available. The only problem is that the decision maker that resides in all of us lives at a deeper level than many of us are naturally predisposed to visit. The decision maker understands that choosing love is certainly one of its options, and it is just as easy to choose love as it is to choose fear. The problem is that it is too easy to get caught up in the everyday drama of life and forget the decision maker even exists. Without encouraging and allowing your decisions to be made at a deeper level, you naturally default to the decisions made by the ego, your small self.

Choosing for love and choosing for peace are the same choice. Unfortunately, the ego has taken over the decision making and the ego is simply a fear-driven machine whose primary purpose is self-perpetuation at any price. The ego is not going to stand idly by while you begin to make decisions with love and peace as the primary motivators rather than the illusions that fear will always provide. Yet most people do not know that

Chapter Two - Make A Commitment To Your Choice

they do, indeed, have a choice, and can circumvent any options the ego is providing. If you get nothing from this book, please walk away from it with the unshakable knowledge that you can and do *always* choose. Every moment of every day is an opportunity to choose either love or fear, peace or turmoil. It is the one power that is exclusively yours.

If you think about it, whether you choose love or fear, peace or turmoil, the energy and brain power necessary to make the choice is the same. However, choosing for love and peace will add to you; it will enhance you and make you stronger; it will expand your thinking and open up vastly new and previously unattainable horizons, and it will bring more of itself to you. Choosing fear, even if this choice is made by the default mechanism of not choosing, will always constrict and severely limit you. It will shrink your thinking and make some level of unsettlement and anxiety your constant companion.

Choose peace today.

Choose Love today.

Make a commitment to your choice.

CHAPTER THREE

THE ILLUSION OF CONTROL

Chapter Three - The Illusion Of Control

"A musician must make music, an artist must paint, a poet must write, if he is to be ultimately at peace with himself."

- *Abraham Maslow*

"Paradise is where I am."

- *Voltaire*

"The great French Marshall Lyautey once asked his gardener to plant a tree. The gardener objected that the tree was slow growing and would not reach maturity for 100 years. The Marshall replied, "In that case, there is no time to lose; Plant it this afternoon."

- *John F. Kennedy*

"Always forgive your enemies. Nothing annoys them so much."

- *Oscar Wilde*

"The last of the human freedoms is our ability to choose our own attitudes."

- *Viktor Frankl*

Chapter Three - The Illusion Of Control

THE PLAN

Aaaahhhh, coffee!

French Roast.

Strong.

The aroma that could only have been given us by benevolent gods wafted through the air and touched gently upon my somewhat sensitive and very thankful olfactory nerves. If I had to wake up at 5:00 in the morning, then I might as well be greeted by the delicious promise that only a freshly brewed pot of strong, dark coffee could offer to an otherwise cobweb-addled brain. The desire for more sleep was always a force to reckon with first thing in the morning, although I am sure the case could be made that 5:00 in the morning was actually the middle of the night. Anybody in his right mind who did not have a really compelling reason to wake up at such an ungodly hour would just turn over and resume snoring, which is exactly what I should have done. But I wasn't in my right mind, so what could be the point?

This was Sunday, a day of rest. It was rumored that even God had chosen to rest on the seventh day. But I was a very important person, a legend in my own mind, and I had some very compelling work to get done. I was also bright enough to understand that the only way to finish anything was to get started and keep going until the job was complete. I was about to engage in what had become a sacred ritual for me, one that occurred every Sunday, whether I liked it or not. It was part of the glue I had manufactured to hold an otherwise very fragile and highly volatile psyche together.

Starting out with a fresh pot of very strong coffee was an absolute necessity for this ritual, and I had found the perfect coffee maker for just such occasions. This incredible little machine not only ground the beans themselves, but I could set an internal timer so that the beans would be ground and the coffee brewed just before my bedside alarm went off. This way, I could awaken with the pleasant and hypnotic invitation that only fresh brewed-coffee can provide. It really helped to jump start my day - and I needed all the help I could get.

Sunday was the day that I spent planning the ensuing week. So what's the big deal, you ask? You get out of bed, a little early perhaps, but you get to work, set out your plan for the week, finish up in a couple of hours, and then you have the rest of the day to yourself. Just think of all the really interesting, creative, and fun ways to spend an entire, responsibility-free day and night. No real jobs to do. No family to take care of. No wives or girl friends hanging around, pushing for me to do this or that. It might even seem worth it to a fairly normal individual to wake up obscenely early on a Sunday, a day that was specifically invented for sleeping late and reveling in sheer laziness. Get the planning done and get on with living a full and rewarding day. Not me. I wasn't a fairly normal individual.

I lived in a 10-room Victorian house with the period details and splendid craftsmanship that only makes you long for the days when people had the time, patience, and talent to take significant pride in doing a fabulous job. Much of the work was not only beautiful; it was downright artistic. I lived in this one-of-a-kind Victorian all by myself. I lived alone in this huge house because I couldn't stand having anyone else around for any appreciable length of time, and I sincerely doubt that any other human being could stand having me around for more than just a few moments either. It was a great place to hide

Chapter Three - The Illusion Of Control

although I didn't know I was hiding at the time. I thought I was some kind of hot shit and that I must really look like a successful businessman if I can afford to live alone in a house like that, all by myself. I was all about appearances.

Actually, I didn't really *live* in this house; I just sort of existed there. Out of a total of 10 rooms, all of which were fully furnished and tastefully decorated, even if I do say so myself, I spent time in only three: the kitchen, my bedroom, and my home office. I lived on Walton Street in Dorchester for a little over two years and, unbeknownst to me this was the time I was going through the very worst of my dry-drunk phase. I slipped further and further into emotional oblivion while working my ass off to hang onto whatever threads of seeming normality I could get my hands on. I was under the mistaken belief that if I made it look good enough for long enough, I would eventually catch up with myself and everything would be ok.

This bit of backwards-living advice came directly and indirectly from my erstwhile therapeutic tag team, and I trusted them because I didn't have anyone else to turn to. I didn't know that there were alternatives and I did not know that I didn't know. My thinking had grown progressively smaller, and the choices available to me as a result had become more limited. So I went with what was in front of me because it was all I knew how to do. And it was slowly killing me.

The tag team had become exceedingly good at living life from the outside-in rather than from the inside-out. They taught that outside appearances and looking good were the most important things to be concerned with. If you lived in a big house, owned more than one house, wore expensive clothes, dropped the right names, went to the right schools, and drove an expensive foreign car, then people would think you were successful. Therefore, you *were* successful. I was under instructions to plan my days very tightly and to then execute the plan. If I did not carry out the plan in a way thought appropriate, then I was to look at what was wrong with me. All of this is the antithesis of living a fulfilled life, a life in which you become the person that God originally intended for you to be. But it was all I had to go on at the time, so I dove in and accepted it as gospel truth.

I was committed to getting better; I wanted to feel like a human being again, and I was willing to do anything in order to achieve these goals. I'm quite sure that I would seriously have considered a lobotomy if someone was able to convince me that it would help. I desperately wanted to reclaim the gentle and innocent boy I once had been. I had made a decision that I was going to heal whatever it was that was wrong with me. I was going to live a fulfilling and rewarding life. I was going to make a difference in the world, and I had made a commitment to that very decision. If it did not work, then I was willing to die trying. I brought every bit of determination and self-discipline I had to the process, which was quite a bit. It was all I knew at the time and I went for it like a drowning man would cling to a life preserver.

So, getting up at five in the morning every Sunday to plan out my week was exactly what I did. But the planning process I engaged in was unlike any that a "normal" person would go anywhere near. I didn't merely sketch an outline for a couple of hours and put it away. I stayed with it until about midnight. That's right. Midnight! I literally spent the entire day, from approximately 5:30 in the morning, which was about the time that the exceedingly strong French Roast coffee began to unravel the cotton that encased my weary brain, until some-

Chapter Three - The Illusion Of Control

where in the vicinity of midnight, planning the upcoming week. I didn't take time out to watch a professional football games, go to a movie, or take myself out to lunch. I didn't provide myself any diversions at all. I moved into my office at home and got to work. The only breaks I took occurred when I ran downstairs to the kitchen, one of the three out of ten rooms I lived in, to make myself something simple to eat, usually a sandwich or a frozen dinner. Thank God for microwave ovens! You really couldn't say that I was a barrel of laughs or a ton of fun to hang out with, but I was committed to getting better, and this was all I knew to do. I didn't know what I didn't know.

You need to remember that this was the late `80s, long before things like hand-held computers or Palm Pilots were available. In fact, I'm pretty certain that time planning software packages had not yet been invented. Even if they existed, I probably would have been too goddamn scared and intimidated to go anywhere near them, because I tend to be somewhat computer-phobic and electronically challenged. Therefore, I used a manual planning system and wrote everything out in longhand. I used the Daytimer system, which, of course, was a recommendation of the often imitated and never duplicated erstwhile therapeutic tag team. The tag team actually ran a seminar they called "The Rainbow Planning Seminar," in which they taught how to make your Daytimer entries with different colors of markers or pens to denote the level of urgency to the task you had written down. Looking good is important, don't you know. If I remember correctly, you were also supposed to use different-colored sticky notes and other stationery paraphernalia to coordinate with the colored entries made in the Daytimer. Of course, they also charged an outrageous fee for this particular brainchild of theirs, and the only people that participated were other people who had been in a therapeutic relationship with them, people over whom they exerted a significant amount of influence.

At the time, the Daytimer Company offered a variety of sizes and layouts, ranging from the very smallest pocket-sized format that provided a different little book for every month of the year, to the granddaddy of them all, an 8 1/2 x 11 three-ring binder type of monster that came with an interesting variety of insert pages and planning tools for the busiest and most important of executive types. That was me! At least in my own mind. Needless to say, I went for the Big Kahuna. I even went for the genuine imitation alligator leather cover. When you are important, when you want to look like you know what you are doing even when you don't, when you want to look good on the outside while the insides are crumbling to desert dust, then you get the biggest and most expensive Daytimer you can find. I also ordered an extra supply of special insert pages, of which I made tons of illegal copies, because I needed much more than the two pages per day a normal person would use for the type of planning I was engaged in.

So there I was, at 5:30 every Sunday morning, me and my Daytimer, me and all those extra insert pages, me and my cup of coffee, planning everything I would do and say for the following week, as well as what anyone else I ran into would say and do, and taking somewhere in the vicinity of eighteen hours to do it! I promise - this actually happened.

I was scared. Fear permeated every cell of my body. I was afraid that if I did not exert control over myself every minute of every day by planning everything in advance, then something very bad was going to happen, because I was very bad to begin with. I believed that I was severely broken, wired for mayhem, and that I came into the world that way. Therefore,

Chapter Three - The Illusion Of Control

if I was going to have a shot at living a somewhat normal existence, then I had to seriously assign myself the task of staying in front of myself, every minute of every day. By extension, then, I had to pre-plan everything that everyone with whom I came in contact would do and say as well, so that I could prepare an adequate response.

You see, I thought I had the ability to control my life because to think otherwise would surely mean that I should just give up and die. It was the thing that kept me from slipping over the edge into whatever oblivion waited for poor unfortunate souls like me who, try as we might, just didn't seem to be able to get it right. I had no idea at that time that the ability to control one's life is actually an illusion. I did not know that my desperate need for control was just another manifestation of the fear that was fueling my engines without my conscious awareness. Much more about this in little while.

When I sat down at my desk every Sunday, I meticulously planned every second of every day of the ensuing week. I painstakingly laid out every conversation I would have with everyone I planned to come into contact with. For every professional appointment I had already scheduled I concocted a strategy for exactly what I would say to whomever I met with what they would say in return. I then decided upon an appropriate response and guessed at their response to my response. Are you beginning to get the picture? Every single word of every conversation I imagined happening would get written down on the special insert pages of which I had so thoughtfully made numerous illegal copies.

I also kept an ongoing list of topics that I felt comfortable talking about so that if I ever found myself in a situation where I had to spend more than a few minutes with somebody, I wouldn't panic for lack of something to say. These situations usually came up if I was having lunch with a customer or found myself in the middle of some kind of a social situation. I often had my topics written down on a small piece of paper stuck in my pocket. If my brain stopped working and I couldn't think of anything with which to fill the dead spots, I would excuse myself, run to the men's room, and study my crib notes when I was convinced nobody was looking. Did anyone ever wonder why I spent so much time in the bathroom?

Monday morning always rolled around with the inevitability of death and taxes. But I was ready. There I was, the proverbial David, walking out the door armed to the teeth with a 700 pound Daytimer, color-coordinated according to the "Rainbow Planning Seminar" rules, to do honest battle with the evil and devious Goliaths of the world. Actually, the whole world seemed like one huge Goliath to me, and running it was no easy task. It only took about two hours into the day on Monday before the whole plan for the week was shot to hell!

One of the definitions of insanity is to keep doing the same things over and over again, but to expect different results. The fact that The Plan never worked in no way gave me the idea to stop doing something that had no hope of success. I never once looked at the reality of the situation and decided to let myself off the hook and allow myself to relax a bit on Sunday. I never once found the slightest bit of humor in the absurdity of what I was trying to do. It never occurred to me that I was wasting a lot of time that could otherwise be spent enjoying myself. And it never dawned on me that what I was attempting to do was actually impossible. The only reaction I had to The Plan's going to hell in a handbasket long before the lunchtime bell sounded on Monday was to work my ass off and make as many fast-paced adjustments as possible. God

Chapter Three - The Illusion Of Control

knows, I certainly had a large enough supply of spare insert sheets to help me in the process. And I would try even harder when Sunday rolled around again and presented me with yet another opportunity to perfect The Plan.

With that being said, let me make one thing perfectly clear, as Richard Nixon was so fond of saying (and the cast of Saturday Night Live was so fond of skewering him for saying): Controlling the world or anything in it for the sake of controlling it was never something I consciously decided to do. I did not sit down one day and notice that the world needed to be run differently and conclude there was no better man for the job than me. I really did not think that highly of myself. The arrogance that I often showed was simply a cover for all the fear, doubt, and insecurity that ruled my inner world. I simply wanted to survive. And The Plan was the only way I knew to accomplish that goal. I know today that such strategy is a little like trying to douse a roaring fire with buckets of gasoline. I succeeded in making myself sicker and sicker. I restricted my thinking to incredibly minute parameters, and I essentially trashed anyone with guts enough to attempt to get close to me.

I am not sure that anyone ever actually sets out to be in control of everything and everyone that crosses their path. Yet on the level of observable behavior, this is exactly what we do, more often than not without knowing we are doing it. And not knowing that we do not know. The illusion of control shows itself in the smaller, day-to-day annoyances and aggravations that surge through your system when things do not go exactly how you think they should, when someone says or does something that doesn't quite conform to your preconceived notion or agenda. Even if said agenda is something of which you are not consciously aware, your feelings are tweaked.

Very simply, you are looking for a certain amount of congruence in your life. Balance. You want to feel good because feeling like a doormat just isn't any fun. You fundamentally understand, at a level much deeper than the conscious one, that the world outside yourself must somehow line up with the world inside. You are simply doing that which ancient instinct tells you to do. Unbeknownst to you, focusing on the outside world as the entity that must change in order to achieve the congruence you seek is backwards and doomed to absolute failure. Been there, done that.

Most people just want to survive, to get by, not cause too much of a stir, to have a little bit of fun, to enjoy family and friends, and generally have the world leave them alone and in peace. But like my favorite author, Stephen King, says in *The Dark Tower* series, "The world has moved on." This isn't Kansas anymore, Dorothy. The world has become much smaller, and living in it has become decidedly more complicated than it was 51 years ago when I took my first breath. The more complicated things become, the greater the perceived need to exert control over the events of our lives, lest they spiral into situations we cannot handle.

I understand now, but did not know then, that seeking for control is a symptom, an outward manifestation of an inner condition. And my inner condition was about as poor and out of control as you could get. I thought that I was broken, that there was something desperately wrong with me, that I had a fundamental flaw in my psyche or personality that would become as clear to everyone as a huge wart on the tip of my nose unless I was able to cover it up by looking good, performing well, and maintaining the facade of a competent and successful professional. Even though I felt like I was really just a bag of shit.

Chapter Three - The Illusion Of Control

I believed that I did not have the ability or the resources to be able to function in the world unless I planned everything out in advance because I thought myself to be a lower-than-cow-dung fraud. I did not trust myself to get through even one day without The Plan because I would end up falling flat on my face and I would expose myself for the impostor that I knew myself to be. What you thought about me was eminently more important than what I thought about me.

The need for control is always driven by fear. Fear permeated every fiber of my being, and I did not know. I was told that anger was my problem. So ridding myself of the ravaging rage that hung around - unwelcome, like a nagging in-law that doesn't seem to want to go away - was the focus of my life. I did not know that anger is always driven by the fear that sits behind it.

I do not recall ever having consciously intended to hurt anybody. Truth be told, I really thought that I had to protect people from me because I was so full of rage I was afraid of what I might do if I did not have a script to follow. In many ways I thought I was dangerous to other people, and one of the benefits of creating The Plan was that I was able to keep myself in check and thereby protect other people from me. I am still trying to figure that one out. I never sought to deprive anyone of any of their basic rights, civil or otherwise. I do not remember actively seeking to limit anyone in any way or interfere with anybody's right to live their life in their own way. But I was crumbling on the inside. I needed to control my life in order to keep myself from permanently falling off the edge, and the only way I knew to get control over my life was to control every aspect of everything in my environment. I needed to direct the orchestra so that nobody would notice that I didn't even know how to read music, let alone play an instrument.

The bottom line is that I was terrified. Fear had permeated me and secured a rather comfortable resting place in every cell of my body, while placing a welcome mat by the door in order to entice even more fear to join the party. The marathon planning session in which I engaged every Sunday was specifically designed to keep myself focused on doing, doing, doing, because I believed right down to the very depths of my being, that if I ever were foolish enough to stop, I would surely die. I was trying in the only way I knew and to the best of my ability, to feel better. The only problem is that, unbeknownst to me, I was going about it in an exactly backwards manner. And I didn't know that I did not know. By going about it "exactly backwards," I mean I struggled to make sure the entire world outside the boundaries of my own skin lined up with my preconceived notions of how things ought to be so that I in turn would feel better inside my own skin. This is how we unconsciously seek balance. I was simply looking to feel better, to find a congruence between the inner and outer worlds. I did not know that the outer world is merely a reflection of the inner condition, and my experience tells me that not very many people do. So I tried to arrange everything and everyone according to how I *thought* they *should* be in order to achieve some semblance of inner peace and happiness.

Living in peace and happiness has always been the goal.

The problem is that my preconceived notions of exactly how things and people *should* be are based only upon that which I had learned, experienced, and been taught since I was a child. This is true for everyone who can fog a mirror, but these notions are generally a very small and often erroneous picture. I worked my ass off first to write the script according to the exceedingly myopic view of the world I had cobbled together from various and sundry resources, and then to

Chapter Three - The Illusion Of Control

direct all the action within my sphere of influence in an ill-fated attempt to feel better. Isn't it always about trying to feel better?

The basic difference between what I did and what most other people do is that I went the extra step of writing the entire script out in my 700 pound Daytimer. Most people walk around with an equally impressive Daytimer, completely written out and color-coordinated, firmly established inside their heads and do not know it is there.

Until I began my study of *A Course In Miracles* I had no idea that all the happiness, love, peace, joy, serenity, harmony, and congruence I so assiduously sought was already mine. I did not know that love and peace were already my true essence and that the place to look for them was right where they always resided and where they reside for you as well - on the inside. I did not know that joy, love, and peace do not have to be *worked for* so much as remembered, recognized, accepted, and given plenty of room to grow.

Look to the inside for the reality of who you are, and the outside will automatically take care of itself!

Chapter Three - The Illusion Of Control

THE VOICE OF THE EGO

I think for the most part people go through life in a somewhat non-deliberate manner, existing from crisis to crisis, managing as best they can, with a little bit of happiness thrown in for good measure. This is most likely because it is the crises that cry out for our attention. We do not seem to have developed an ability to define our lives by that which is right, that which feels good, that which creates peace and harmony every day. You might as well just admit it - you are often eminently more comfortable in the familiar midst of an active shitstorm than you are in feeling at peace. As long as there doesn't get to be a significant problem or series of significant problems, you seem to be able to manage, to get by, to stay just enough ahead of the pack of wolves that is constantly nipping at your heels so that a huge chunk does not get bitten out of your backside. The goal is to keep the internal pinball machine from reading *tilt* and shutting all systems down rather than seeking to live a supremely fulfilling and meaningful life. Getting by seems to be good enough.

In living that way, you are unwittingly listening to the voice of the ego, the small self that really is not a self at all. The ego tells you that in order to find the balance you seek, you must be in control of your life. On the surface this is an argument that makes some sense. However, it is an extremely skillful misdirection, not unlike that which has been used by magicians since the dawn of time to convince us that what they are doing is the real deal. Similarly, the ego logically points you to the things in your life that need to be fixed and tells you that all you need to do is work harder, apply more effort, put the hammer down a little bit stronger, and everything will be as you would like. But the ego does not tell you that there is a slight side effect that goes along with trying to take control of your life and it is that you must also exert a certain amount of control over the other people in your life. If the ego allowed you to focus on that which is right, it would atrophy and die because it wouldn't have anything to do.

Remember, the ego seeks to maintain its existence at all costs and does so by ensuring that you never find the peace you are looking for. So you end up living your life from one situation to the next until they all get strung together, one virtually indistinguishable from the other, into a long line of energy-draining stressors. They chip away at your happiness, curtail the simple enjoyment you might otherwise get out of life, and undermine your attempts to build real and long-lasting relationships.

When you listen to and respond to the voice of the ego, you experience a constant low hum on the inside, a prevalent discord, a feeling that something isn't exactly how it ought to be. There is a piece missing in the puzzle and you don't know exactly where to find it. You look everywhere, more often than not unaware that you are looking. You are also not always consciously aware of the constant buzz, the internal message that something just doesn't line up here. But you see the results of this internal unrest in your reactions to other people - the brief flashes of anger and resentment that flare up when people do not do what you expect. Perhaps your wife is late getting the dinner ready, and you respond with anger and silent disapproval. Or perhaps a co-worker gets a promotion that you sincerely believe should have been yours, and you change the way you behave toward her. You see it in the immediacy and intensity of your reaction when another driver cuts you off on the highway, when the burger you buy at McDonald's is cold or under cooked, when someone tells you they are going to do something and you count on it and it does

Chapter Three - The Illusion Of Control

not happen, or when you seem to hit every red light on the planet while driving to an appointment for which you started out later than planned because you were distracted by handling yet another family mini-crisis.

Every single human being experiences an adverse internal reaction whenever something doesn't go exactly according to plan, even if you are not consciously aware of having a plan. It is endemic to the human condition, and there isn't a person on the planet who is immune to this particular malady. Someone else does or says something (or you perceive that someone else has thought or felt something you think is inappropriate) that doesn't quite line up with what you want or expect them to say, do, think or feel and you experience a shift in *your* internal equilibrium.

Like water seeks its own level, you have a level of internal balance that you seek to maintain. As soon as that sense of balance is threatened, alarm bells begin to ring, some more loudly than others, depending on the perceived severity of the stimulus. It reminds me of the robot on the old television series *Lost In Space*. Whenever some cleverly conceived alien menace threatened the Robinson family, the robot would run around with his arms flailing and yell out in his mechanical voice, " DANGER! DANGER! DANGER"!

Once the threat is perceived, you automatically begin the search for counter measures and you look for those measures on the external radar screen, which is the wrong place to look. You have unfortunately been preprogrammed through thousands of years of genetic engineering to fight or flee in response to any external stimulation that isn't entirely congruent with whatever exists internally. You will instinctively seek to remain in the state of balance that you have deemed tolerable for you. This instinct is so automatic that you are generally unaware that your survival mechanism has even been activated. You will always seek this balance even if you are not consciously aware of doing so. However, the "balance' you are working so hard to maintain is simply a leveling-out process between the crises of the moment. The real goal is to ensure that the highs don't get too high nor the lows too low. Emotional mediocrity then becomes a way of life.

The point I am trying to make is that while your thoughts, feelings, and behaviors are being dictated and driven by the infinitesimal ego-mind on the surface level, your Real Self - the part of you that is not a part at all because it is all of you - is always very patiently calling you to come home. Your entire life is a battle dedicated to finding and maintaining a sense of balance that your ego tells you is possible to achieve. But the only way to achieve it is to have the whole world march in lock-step to the cadence you dictate. This is an impossible task, a little like Sysiphus doomed to an eternity of pushing his boulder up a hill. The only answer is to connect yourself to the Peace of God, which already exists inside and from which you were originally created. Balance is just another word for peace. Therefore, it is peace that you truly seek.

Living life from the inside out means that the voice of the ego becomes a very distant and faint echo, unable to exert much influence in your life at all. Living life from the inside out means never having to be in charge again.

Chapter Three - The Illusion Of Control

THE PRE-EMPTIVE STRIKE

As I mentioned before, seeking a sense of balance in our lives, whether we do it by conscious decision or not, is something we are all wired for. The voice for God never entirely goes away, no matter how bad we think we are. It is always there, gently calling us home. If you are anything like me, and I believe you are, you sometimes go to some fairly interesting extremes to achieve a sense of balance. It is a fairly common experience, for instance, to engage in what could be considered some sort of pre-emptive strike. This is when you adjust your behavior or attitude in anticipation of someone else doing or saying something that doesn't exactly coincide with your version of the written script. How many time have you been driving home having an argument in your head with your wife, husband, or children, long before you open the door in greeting?

This internal dialog usually runs through every possible permutation of the argument in your head. The general theme often has to do with getting your way about some current issue in which you have cast yourself in the role of either the misunderstood victim or the savior of the family's life and sanity. All angles of your internal diatribe lead to the end result of you sitting comfortably on your diamond-studded throne, safely in charge of the kingdom once again, another attempted insurrection by the home-based cast of lowly minions having successfully been put down, and blessed order - your version of blessed order, having thankfully been restored.

One of the interesting things you will notice about having these arguments, fights, spats, or disagreements with people long before you have a chance to actually speak to them directly is that the longer the thing lives in your head, the more agitated, upset, angry, of fearful you become. You are actually reacting to your thoughts as though they are real, as though the poisonous scenario you have been creating in your own head has already occurred. You can feel your level of tension increase; you are either anticipating the absolute worst or you have formulated a vision of a very difficult encounter. *And nothing has happened yet!*

Either way, you are definitely ready for some kind of confrontation and are generally so full of righteous indignation that nothing is going to deter you from setting things straight. I know that you can relate to what I am saying because, to a greater or lesser extent, everybody does it. Nobody is immune to the condition of being human. Everybody on the face of the planet pre-plans arguments, fights, and disagreements that are either directly related to the lightning-rod issues of the moment or elaborate diversions from those issues.

I am absolutely clear that you have had the experience of playing out a fight you would like to have with another individual - could be a family member, boss, coworker, a member of your church, or the President of The United States - without actually having an interaction with the other person. Personally, I have been enjoyed many of these heated internal discussions with various presidents over the years, and I can assure you that the world would be in much better condition if only they had the courage enough to listen to me and then to perfectly carry out my infallible instructions. Someday, perhaps...

At any rate, I also know that you can relate to your feelings changing in direct proportion to the intensity of the confrontation occurring inside your head. Unfortunately, the next thing that happens is that you arrive at your destination feeling and behaving like a runaway nuclear warhead, seeking to lay waste

Chapter Three - The Illusion Of Control

to whatever is in your heat-seeking path and totally unwilling to take any prisoners. Or you put on a happy face and pretend that nothing is going on with you, only to subsequently berate yourself unmercifully for being such a jelly fish for never opening your mouth and saying what is on your mind. Whereupon, the only thing you are able to think about, the only thing that will appear on the radar screen you otherwise call conscious thought, the only information your now-diminished capacity for critical thinking can possibly process, is that which you were too chickenshit to say. Either way, you lose.

An alternative approach, one that would increase the level of peace you experience in your everyday life, would be first to simply notice what you are doing when the aforementioned mental diatribes are occurring. Look at the thoughts that are swirling around inside your head, *without judging yourself for having the thoughts in the first place,* and decide to make a change. Make yourself stop the conversation by whatever means works for you. Changing the subject could be an effective beginning. It is also very helpful if you make yourself look at the situation from the other person's perspective, a skill that anyone can develop with a little bit of willingness.

Changing your mind is something that is actually within your power, something you really do have control over, something that will make you feel better rather than worse, and something that can make an immediate difference in your perception of the world in which you live.

I am not saying that it is easy, but it is a place to start. It is like everything else - the more you practice, the more effective you will become. Try to imagine an entirely different way of looking at the situation that has you so riled up. Look at it from another person's point of view. Give weight to their arguments without merely dismissing them out of hand. Allow yourself to entertain a reasonable doubt that you may not be entirely correct, that you may not have all of the pertinent facts after all. At least you can remind yourself that you do not have the big picture, which means that you do not know for sure why this situation is in your life to begin with. Resolve to learn any lessons that are currently being taught. And try to forgive yourself for being so impetuous. It would also be a good idea to forgive the other person, too because, as we have seen, nothing has happened.

I remember a time when I was living in Stow and I was having a fight with my wife. I am not sure what the disagreement was about, but I can safely assume it was one that I started after having completely fabricated whatever issue happened to be on the table. I swear, Elaine probably should have walked around wearing a suit of protective armor back then, because she never knew from which direction I was going to launch the next assault. I remember recognizing that I was way off base, that I had some things definitely mixed up. I was, once again, off on another one of my little tangents. I remember muttering something akin to an apology before retreating to the basement to lick my wounds. Think about it! I started the fight and I am heading to the basement to lick *my* wounds?

But wait, it gets better! I sat there in the downstairs bathroom and thought about what just happened. I realized I was mistaken. I had some things mixed up. I knew the best thing in the world for me to do when I walked back upstairs was to keep my mouth shut and give us enough time to get through this little episode. I concluded that forgetting all about what I imagined the problem to be, changing the subject as it were, before going back upstairs, would be a very intelligent and

Chapter Three - The Illusion Of Control

practical thing to do. So, armed with my new determination to replace the anxiety I had previously aroused with calm and level-headed behavior, I went upstairs and promptly began the fight all over again.

Such is the pull, the attraction, of the need to be in control. And such is the damage we can cause when we seek to fulfill that need.

Nobody wants to be known as a "control freak." We all know people who fall into this category and nobody likes to hang around with them. Many people seem to take such a mission to interesting levels, and they just aren't any fun. But every time you seek to get something your way because you know it is the "right" way, even if you don't consciously say those words to yourself, you are looking to exercise control. Every time you have one of those high-intensity (or even low-intensity) internal dialogs with someone else, you are exercising your "right" to be the captain of the ship. Every time you adversely react to a particular situation in your life and unconsciously bring that energy to bear in another unrelated incident - more determined to have it your way in one arena because you just lost it in another - you are looking to be in control.

And there is nothing wrong with this other than the fact that you are spending precious time and energy in pursuit of a goal that can never be realized. Like I said, it is impossible to be immune from the condition of being human. The important thing is that you begin to recognize your own propensity to be in control, in whatever forms it may be manifest, because that is a very important first step in releasing yourself from the prison you have created and allowing yourself to begin realizing a life of tranquility and peace. Control is an illusion. It is not possible, and every second that is spent in pursuit of a goal that cannot be reached is time and energy that can be used in endeavors that are not predestined to end in frustration, anger, and further discomfort.

Make no mistake about it. Every time you seek to be in control of anything, you are driven by fear and you have become the architect, engineer, and construction crew of an invisible wall separating you from your Real Self, as well as the rest of humanity.

Fear is the culprit.

THE UNCOVERED TOOTHPASTE

Let's look at very silly example. You get up in the morning and walk on wobbly legs, misty-eyed and barely awake, into the bathroom to take care of certain mandatory biological functions. As you begin to focus a little bit more clearly, you notice, there on the vanity, right before your very eyes, sitting boldly in plain sight, is the uncapped tube of toothpaste. You also can't help but notice the contents have already dripped onto what would otherwise have been a perfectly pristine vanity surface, and you feel that familiar knot tighten in your belly just before a minor explosion rips through head. You have been down this road before. You have expressed your extreme displeasure of uncapped toothpaste tubes on more than one occasion, and you see this uncapped and dripping tube of Tom's of Maine toothpaste as a personal rebuke.

There will be hell to pay. Anger and righteous indignation race through your suddenly and rudely awakened system as you struggle between some prudently acceptable and some not-so-subtle, in-your-face type of ways to register your disbelief to the particular non-conforming individual in question. Unbeknownst to you, it is fear that has gone screaming through your heretofore relatively calm system and driven the anger that you are experiencing at such a heightened level.

You are losing control!

Within a nanosecond you completely understand the problem is not just the tube of toothpaste. The devastation has been widespread, and you have been remiss in your duties. You immediately picture the dirty dish left in the sink last week, the bed that was so inconsiderately left unmade the other day, and the dirty socks casually thrown on the floor of the closet just yesterday. All the telltale signs are there. Your world is falling apart, and you have to do something about it.

You are losing control.

In reality the toothpaste tube is not the problem, and the other person is not the problem, either. They have simply served as the lightening rods for the fear that already existed inside you, albeit somewhat dormant. As soon as the fear is ignited, your ego undertakes an exercise in damage control and begins a deep memory scan and perimeter check to determine where there may have been other breaches of protocol. You instinctively know that the problem doesn't stop with just the toothpaste. Where there is one, there is bound to be more than one. You may well need this tank of gasoline to throw on the fire of the ensuing encounter in order to more dramatically prove your point. And so the pre-fight internal dialog begins anew, never having gone very far away for very long. Same shit, different day.

The offending party, in the meantime, is off doing whatever he does in the morning, going about his business, whistling a happy tune, completely unaware of the volcano that is erupting in another room. Out of sight, out of mind. He has in no way been impacted by the fact that he left the toothpaste uncovered. It is not on his radar screen; it never once entered his mind. It was not an act of willful defiance; he was simply thinking about his ensuing day while he brushed his teeth and just happened to have left the bathroom without covering the toothpaste tube. No big deal. He is perfectly happy to cover that old tube of Tom's of Maine in order to keep the peace because he knows that you have attached such significance to it, but it doesn't really matter to him at all. He never gives it one second of consideration, it is a non-issue.

Chapter Three - The Illusion Of Control

He has simply forgotten to cover the tube, and his forgetting has nothing whatsoever to do with you. It doesn't even have anything to do with him. It doesn't mean anything. It is a simple oversight. He understands that the quality of his life is neither positively nor negatively affected by whether or not the toothpaste tube is covered - except that he has experienced the ration of rudeness that comes his way whenever he commits such an egregious offense. He is free. You, on the other hand, are trapped, as much a prisoner in a cell of your own making as any convicted felon who is living as a guest of the government in an institution where actual steel bars place the limitations on a person's physical freedom. The uncovered tube of toothpaste in and of itself does not mean anything. It is you who bestow meaning upon it.

Any time you have a preconceived notion of what *ought* to occur, how another person or institution *should* behave, exactly what is or is not acceptable performance by someone else, what someone else *should or should not* think or feel, you have attached some degree of emotional significance to a scenario that you have invented. You have also erected another board in the fence that barricades you from feeling the fresh air and sunshine of freedom and life. This is often called *"shoulding"* all over yourself.

The expectation belongs to you because it came from you. Therefore, the angst, frustration, anger, and fear you feel as a result of something not going according to your predetermined notions, is a direct result of your notion, not of the other person's failure to follow your plan. Think about it: If the notion did not exist, then the resultant anger could not be possible and you would not feel so lousy. It has been well said that expectations are resentments looking for a place to happen. So the answer lies in looking at yourself - not someone

161

else - as the source of your own discomfort. This is good news because you can actually do something about changing your own perspectives and preconceived notions, but you can't do one blessed thing to change someone else.

Another individual walking into the bathroom may not even notice that the toothpaste is uncovered. It is not important to her. It does not affect the quality of her life in any way. This is because she has not attached any meaning at all to whether the toothpaste is covered or uncovered. It is a non-issue.

In the case of our silly example, you need to ask yourself why covering the tube of toothpaste is so important to you. You need to keep on asking until you get an answer. And the answer has ONLY to do with you. It is all about you. If you find yourself focusing on anyone else in your answer, start again. Of course, this is just one silly little example, but you can apply the same technique to any situation in your life.

Let's face it: We often have scripts written for other people to follow and never bother to inform them that such a script exists. A technicality such as this doesn't seem to matter because it works for you when someone does not perform according to your plan. It generates anger and at some level you *want* to be angry; you have a right to your anger. You have become accustomed to the presence of some degree of anger simmering in your system. It is familiar. You want to feel like you have been disrespected because a proper blast of good old-fashioned righteous indignation gets the blood boiling, makes you feel alive. Could it be, then, that you actually set up a situation to produce the poisonous feelings inside because they are so familiar that living without them actually feels like you are dying? Been there, done that. You have to die to the old in order to live to the new.

THE REAL DEAL

Sometimes you don't even know that your own personal script for everyone else's performance exists because you are blindly following along according to what you have learned growing up and have not questioned. You may well have been taught from the time you were a very little girl that covering the tube of toothpaste is polite, considerate, and all that is acceptable. It then logically follows that anyone who leaves the toothpaste uncovered is impolite, inconsiderate, and unacceptable. Rather than thinking freely, your visceral reaction to the uncovered tube of toothpaste is a direct result of training, of attaching a meaning and a resultant emotional load to the object that it does not posses in and of itself.

The meaning and judgment come from you, not the toothpaste nor the offending party. This is the good news because you then have the power to change your perspective - which does not consciously occur to you once the adrenaline begins to course through your veins. It is not surprising when you take this internal conflict to its next logical level and conclude that he couldn't possibly love you if he behaves in such an obviously unloving way. You have placed yourself at the center of his universe - the cause and effect of his thoughts, feelings, and behaviors.

The next step is the BIG one. The real deal. Once you have adequately seen that the emotional wringer you have gone through as a result of the uncovered toothpaste tube has nothing to do with anyone else but you - once you can own it - you can then FORGIVE him for the mistake you have made. This one is so important, I will say it again:

You can forgive him for the mistake <u>YOU</u> have made.

This is real forgiveness because it releases both of you simultaneously. This approach can and does work for any situation you find yourself in, no matter what. If you take nothing else from this book, take this and let it become part of you. Real forgiveness, as described above, will release you from the bonds of your judgments and expectations, and it will release everyone else in your life from those same bonds. This forgiveness assumes we do not see the big picture, that we do not know why a certain situation has been brought into our lives. It assumes that our perceptions are very limited and driven by past erroneous perceptions, and it assumes that we often react to situations with very little actual data on the table.

Real forgiveness assumes that if we are impacted by something in an adverse manner, at least part of that adverse reaction has been created by us, and our automatic impulse is to place the blame elsewhere. Therefore, real forgiveness occurs whenever we can forgive other people for the mistakes we have made. It is very powerful!

It is forgiveness that will set you free. The ability to forgive other people for the mistakes you have made will change your life immediately and forever. Acquiring the ability to do so will grant you the peace you so truly deserve and for which you have searched so long.

Chapter Three - The Illusion Of Control

CONTROL IS AN ILLUSION

It is impossible to become an adult in the world today and not have a whole corporation's worth of preconceived notions that you picked up over the years without even knowing it. When this occurs, you find yourself getting angry at someone without completely understanding why, and you naturally look to place the responsibility for your feelings on the other person. Clearly, he must have done or said something to piss you off. No. Your feeling comes from you, not the other person. It is only about you. Honest self-examination, looking inside rather than outside, will provide you with the answers you seek. The trick is to make yourself stop and take a look.

I understand that this is a difficult concept to grasp initially because it is diametrically opposed to most of what you have learned in your life, and it feels very uncomfortable when you first begin the process. Looking inside rather than outside for your answers is very awkward and fear evocative at first. It feels a little like deciding to learn how to swim after a lifetime of being afraid of the water. But it is paramount that you begin because it is the **only** way to achieve the happiness you are looking for. Therefore, it is both a good idea and a positive, life-enhancing step, to begin to view those times when you feel even slightly uncomfortable about something as an opportunity to learn something about yourself. Turn the negative in your thinking into the positive that it really is. The answers that you seek are inside, not outside.

If you do not develop the skill of looking at yourself as the source of your discomfort in any situation, your life will go along as it always has up to this point, and nothing substantial will change. You will enjoy many moments of anger, frustration, fear, and desperation, with some feelings of peace and happiness thrown in for good measure every now and again. If you do develop the skill of looking inside rather than outside for your answers, then happiness, joy, serenity, and peace will become a way of life for you. Forgiveness is possible when you finally realize that the problem begins with you.

Forgiveness, real forgiveness, is the key to the kingdom.

The point is that you have created a prison for yourself and you don't even know it. You cannot successfully control anything outside the boundaries of your own skin, but you have some fairly specific notions as to exactly how things should occur. Anytime something doesn't happen according to the greater plan you have devised, whether consciously or unconsciously, you are the one that feels the pain. This must tell you that if The Plan did not exist, the pain would not come. You are the screenwriter, author, producer, director, and featured star of your very own psychodramatic mini-series, and the inevitable outcome is not the happy and glorious endings you love to see in the movies. Your mini-drama will always end in feelings of anger, fear, frustration, aggravation, and loneliness for you. It cannot happen any other way unless you are willing to live without the screenplay. You must be willing to live without The Plan, and trust that you will be carried, because you have always been carried. You just do not realize it yet.

Control of any kind is an illusion.

I do not know of one other human being who has taken the development of The Plan to the extent that I did. I don't know one other person who has actually spent somewhere in the vicinity of seventeen hours every Sunday creating The Plan for the ensuing week. I can honestly tell you that I have been there, done that, and it does not work. I have learned that it

Chapter Three - The Illusion Of Control

doesn't matter whether you spend sixteen hours, six hours, or six minutes - if your planning is driven by fear as mine was and has controlling your life as its central theme (remember, you cannot control your own life without trying to control everyone and everything around you) you have embarked on a magnificent exercise in abject self-deception that cannot possibly work. Even if you spend *six seconds*, whether consciously or unconsciously, developing plans or scripts for other people, you are wasting your time and building the bars of your own personal prison.

Today my planning is very different. I generally sit down for a period of time on Sundays and write a list of the things I need to get done during the week. I then take a little time to prioritize these tasks so I make sure I get to the most important ones. My planning has only to do with me. It helps me remember that I need to do certain things because as soon as the work week begins I can be pulled in many different directions. I need something to remind me of the tasks that I determine are the most important because I can be easily side tracked. My planning is direction-setting in nature rather than control-gathering. I am much more interested in keeping myself on the track I determine is the one I want to be on rather than making sure everyone else is on my track. Then I let it go and allow myself to be carried in the direction that feels like the one God is choosing, which is just another way of saying that I have also learned the importance of letting go of the results. Occasionally, Sunday comes and goes and I don't even write a list.

Think about it another way. What is your general reaction whenever you perceive that someone else is trying to control or manipulate you? How do you feel when someone or something else is looking to limit your personal freedom, trying to *make* you think or feel a certain way, making all the rules to suit themselves, or telling you that what you really think or feel is either wrong, inappropriate, or unacceptable? What does it feel like when you are being limited by forces outside yourself? What does it feel like when someone else has written the screenplay and you are supposed to blindly follow along and unquestioningly read your lines, without who you really are being involved? What does it feel like to be on the receiving end of someone else's nasty attitude and resentment because you did not blindly adhere to the agenda he created for you, one that he never bothered to tell you about and which he simply assumed you *should* know? It feels horrible!!! You feel unappreciated, belittled, angry, outraged, and frustrated. You feel like you really do not matter, like there is nothing you can do or say that is correct. Every time you try you get beaten down, so what's the point?

If you feel this way when someone or something else has written your script, how do you think it makes someone else feel when you are the author and director. Well that's different, says the ego, automatically. You really *do* know what is right and you really *do* know the best thing. You tell yourself you are really always thinking of everyone else's best interests. However, upon closer and honest self-examination, you will find that your agenda is self-serving. Yet the truth is that your interests would be much better served without seeking control of any kind. You will much more easily live to your greatest potential, achieve the goals that have for so long been unattainable dreams, and begin to feel a congruence between the inside and outside worlds that is very peaceful indeed.

Also, if you can accept that you often have a script in place for other people to follow and don't know it, it is quite possible that whenever someone else has a script prepared for you, he

Chapter Three - The Illusion Of Control

does not know it either. Therefore, you can forgive him for, "he knows not what he does." Forgiveness will set you free.

The ego will always seek to justify the unjustifiable and it will always look outward for its focus. The ego knows that if you begin to look inward what you must eventually and inevitably stumble upon a very small piece of the truth, the antithesis of that which the ego stands for. The ego further surmises that as soon as you find one single sliver of the Truth and recognize it for what it is, you will begin to apply what you learned to every aspect of your life because it is the only thing that makes sense. Then the ego's demise is all but inevitable. Make no mistake about it: the ego will fight you to maintain control and will give you every excuse you will ever need to keep you from making the changes that will diminish its power over you. But it is a fight that the ego cannot win.

THE MACROCOSM AND
THE MICROCOSM ARE THE SAME

I mentioned in Chapter One that every organism in the entire universe works according to the exact same principles. Whether it is a planet, government, non-profit agency, corporation, individual, family, or single cell in your body, the governing principles are the same. Think about it. Whenever certain cells in your body attack and destroy other cells, the result is sickness, disease, and death. So too in the sphere of human interaction.

To emphasize the point about controlling behavior being a waste of energy and never producing the desired results of happiness or peace, let's take a look at international dynamics. These are somewhat removed from the immediacy of our personal lives and therefore provide the safety of distance with which we can begin some of these concepts. Remember, though, that the exact same dynamics apply to international relationships as apply to your personal life. You can seamlessly apply the lessons from the international level to your personal life, and vice versa. According to *A Course In Miracles,* there is no degree of difficulty in miracles. Therefore, there is no degree of difficulty in error. One nation trying to conquer another nation is the same as one human being trying to control the next.

Never in the course of human history has a government or nation survived that has been built on the backs of its people or by conquering and subjugating the people of another nation. It has **NEVER** succeeded and it never will. Read as many history books as you would like or watch The History Channel from dawn to dusk, and you will not find a single example where it has worked. Not one. The Roman Empire eventually suffered a very long and painful death. Napoleon's vision of French world domination was cut dramatically short by the combined forces of the Russian winter and the fierce determination of an indigenous population refusing to be subjugated by a foreign despot. Hitler's Thousand Year Reich lasted a mere thirteen years, and the planned conquest of the Middle East by George W. Bush will certainly teach him that it would be a good idea to at least open a history book and notice that such domination was already attempted by the Romans, Turks, Russians, British, Arabs, French, and Germans, as well as armies of Crusaders, Moors, and Sarazens. All totally without success.

Like I said, a superbly appropriate definition of insanity is doing the same things over and over again but expecting different results.

Any national leader who believes that he or she will be the first one in the history of man to successfully force whatever his notion of how a government *should* be run on another country or how that population *should* go about living life, is listening to the voice of the ego and is sorely mistaken. Any compelling "justifications" there may seem to be, such as national security or self-defense, are really only very old and worn out variations on the same theme of fear-driven and ego-centric grabs for power. Ego-driven fear will always be the cause of any decision by the people of one nation to conquer or in any way attempt to subjugate the people of another nation, and the human race has been reliving the same symptoms of the cause forever. It's a little like Bill Murray's character in the movie *Groundhog Day* reliving the same day over and over and over again. The big difference is that the movie is really funny. And Bill Murray is great!

Chapter Three - The Illusion Of Control

The reason that successful long-term subjugation of another race, religion, or people simply cannot work is that the entire notion is based on lies. We are lying to ourselves whenever we believe we are better than someone else, that our way is the only way, or that someone else is wrong because he or she does something differently than we do. We are lying to ourselves if we believe we are inherently any better or any worse than anyone else on the face of the planet because everybody, everywhere - from the primitive tribes of the Amazon rain forest to the blue-blood scholars plying the hallowed halls of Harvard University, is a child of God and therefore equal. Our collective reality, a reality that we are powerless to change whether we like it or not, is that we are all an extension of God Himself, and God cannot be any better or any worse than Himself. Pure and simple, any activity based on a lie cannot be sustained. This is why conquest has never and will never work. It is why war has never and will never work. And it is why the only reasonable answer is peace.

The justifications for international aggression usually appear in the guise of national security or self-defense. These are really only creative spins placed on the underlying desires for personal, financial, political, or economic gain. Telling ourselves that we are invading another nation to free the people is pure hogwash because nobody ever makes decisions that they do not first perceive to be in their own self interest. The interesting thing is that the aforementioned goals of personal, financial, political, or economic gain **CAN** be achieved - and in significantly more abundance than could ever be imagined - within an atmosphere of peace and without ever having to fire a single shot. Peace can free individuals and entire populations to be dramatically more creative and productive. Peace and possibility are the best economic motivators imaginable.

The same principles apply, dare I say, to organized religions. Countless wars have been fought in the name of one god or another. When you get right down to the nitty-gritty this is really just one religious group making itself better in its own eyes by making the other guys appear worse. At the bare-bones level it is the same thing as one person justifying his position by un-justifying someone else's. Words and concepts such as "heathen" and "infidel" are used when we are being critical of other religions, ridiculing their practices and beliefs, and deciding that its practitioners *should* therefore be converted, by force if necessary. The Spanish Conquistadors "converted" millions of indigenous people in the New World by killing them. That'll show 'em.

It is a classic. You can't make yourself the "best" or "the good guy" without making someone else the "worst." It is the same dynamic as when one person belittles another person in an altogether backwards and totally ineffective attempt to make himself feel better about himself. Remember, the answers are inside and *never* have to do with anything or anyone else. In the case of organized religions, I think it would make things much easier and a whole lot less messy if the various Gods who are worshiped throughout the world would just get together in some remote location, perhaps in the Sahara Desert, smoke a peace pipe, and retire from active duty.

On an international level, we don't seem to have learned that the mightiest armies in the world are not as powerful as that which lives in the heart of a single man. Seeking to force change upon, or in any way subjugate, another race, religious group, or nation is exactly the same as trying to control another individual. The effort is always driven by fear, and it is always doomed to failure.

Chapter Three - The Illusion Of Control

We never have control. All we ever have is an illusion of control.

Scan the history books and you will find that what I am saying is true. The Soviet Empire has disintegrated, and the Berlin Wall has been reduced to chunks of concrete that you can purchase on E-bay and hang in your living room. The once mighty British Empire has vanished, and England has never (and will never) regain the degree of influence it was once able to simply force on the people of the nations it invaded and conquered. The Catholic Church is crumbling from within in the wake of worldwide sexual scandals and the continued mistaken presumption that it has the right to dictate morality to members of the church while refusing to accept the same standard of conduct for itself. Talking the talk instead of walking the talk, as it were.

The American Civil war was a brutal conflagration that was fought to eradicate slavery. Yet this altogether repugnant institution is but a symptom of the racial intolerance and prejudice that are the by-products of fear and ignorance. The eradication of slavery did not eliminate the cause of slavery. The effect never leaves unless the cause is removed, and removing one form of the effect (slavery) without eliminating its cause (fear and ignorance) simply means that it will show itself in another way. Until fear is replaced by unconditional love and acceptance, the human race will always experience the effects of racial, religious, and ethnic hatred.

The fact of the matter is that the American Founding Fathers had an opportunity to write anti-slavery legislation into the U. S. Constitution, but they were too scared to enter the debate for fear of losing the nation that was just coming together. Fear of any outcome, no matter how large or small it is perceived to be, will significantly influence any decision that is being made unless the darkness of fear is brought to the light of truth. The Founding Fathers decided that they would not even debate the question of slavery, which eliminated the possibility of shedding the light of truth on the subject. A mere two generations later, the nation was torn apart by the million-pound gorilla that was left sitting in the middle of the living room, unacknowledged and very hungry.

Once again, putting an end to slavery merely eliminated one of the outward manifestations of racism. It eliminated one of a million possible effects but never touched the cause. The cause is fear, and the antidote is acceptance and unconditional love, the basis of living a life of peace. The only way this can be accomplished on a worldwide level is one person at a time, one day at a time, one thought at a time.

You cannot legislate that which any person chooses to allow to live in his or her own heart. Conquering a nation, race, or religion never entirely conquers the people because it cannot be done. A person's heart is entirely un-conquerable. The same is true for interpersonal relations.

Your job is to identify any and all unacknowledged fears you might have and ask God to help you understand them. Place your fears entirely in His hands with the same urgency with which you would drop a hot coal, and ask Him to help you shed the burden of carrying this load. You will be amazed at the transformation that will take place in your life every day. All of the answers for you, every single one, in every aspect of your life, already exist inside. The easiest and safest way to access them is to ask for help from Him who gave them to you in the first place.

I truly believe that the burgeoning American Empire which

Chapter Three - The Illusion Of Control

seeks to force its brand of democracy on the people of other countries because of the mistaken belief that "we know what is best for them" is destined to go the way of so many other pretentious powers. We delude ourselves with the erroneous notion that the people of other nations really long for American Democracy even if they are not actually asking us to give it to them. We tell ourselves that they need American Democracy in order to survive even if they do not seem to know this clearly unassailable fact. After all, hasn't it worked well for America?

Take the exact same line of thought and simply change the form in which it has been used by countless nations and religions since the dawn of man, and you will see that it is simply more of the same self-delusional rhetoric that has always resulted in death, destruction, devastation, and suffering. It doesn't matter what level of emotion and reaction the political spin doctors are able to generate; it doesn't matter the angle at which some sort of believable justification is seen; it doesn't matter how palatable the rhetoric gets to be. It is ultimately all the same pack of lies that one leader or another has been selling to the people of their nations or religions since the days of Cro Magnon man and before. And the result has always been the same!

The result will always be the same until a true leader one day stands up and says; "No matter what, I am going to wage peace." This is the eternal position, one that is beyond the minutiae of day-to-day worries and concerns, one that is untouched by the prejudices and fears of the small mind as it seeks to make you its prisoner and the world your jailer, and one that is untouched by the constantly shifting machinations that are so endemic to the human species. It is also a position that any nation or individual can measure any pending decision against by asking a very simple question. Will this bring me peace? If the answer is yes, then give it a go. If the answer is no, then find something else to do that will bring peace.

It is critical for you to understand that accepting nothing short of peace in your life is **NOT** in any way a position of weakness. Quite the contrary, it is the position of ultimate strength and power. It emanates from a direct connection to the eternal power of God and cannot be touched by any man.

You will have peace and abundance in your life the day you decide that, no matter what, you are going to have peace. This peace can be experienced as a way of life, every day, for the rest of your life, no matter what kind of turmoil swirls around you and no matter what anyone else says or does. Peace, love, joy, and serenity already belong to you, although you do not know that yet. You have always had them and you always will. There is absolutely nothing you can do to change that because it is the peace of God with which you were created long before you took your first mortal breath. The peace and love of God are your true self, your real essence. All you need to do is accept this, remember it, and decide it is all you will allow to exist in your life. This is a decision you *do* have control over and one that you certainly have the power to make. Decide for peace. Today!

Remember, insanity is doing the same things over and over again but expecting different results.

EXAMPLES OF REAL-LIFE DECISIONS FOR PEACE

Just as making peace the only acceptable alternative on an international level would bring about the safety, prosperity, and growth that people of the world have been seeking for half of forever, living from a foundation of inner peace on a personal level would intrinsically bring the congruence that you seek. If everybody on the planet one day decided to live from a platform of peace, then war, racism, intolerance, and economic hardship would, like the bubonic plague that once so powerfully threatened to exterminate the world population, forever disappear.

A very good step toward realizing a life of peace is to identify all of the people, places, and things you would bend to your will and begin the process of handing the responsibility for running the world over to God, or whatever notion of a higher power you may have. I find it much more effective to begin this process using whomever you have designated as your greatest tormentor. Please entertain the notion that you really do not have control. All you have is the illusion of control, and every minute you spend trying to have things your way actually diminishes your experience of peace and serenity rather than adds to them.

You only have control over the decisions you make. You can decide how you will interpret your life and everything in it, one day at a time and one thought at a time.

Please understand that I am not trying to stake out any particular political point of view. I am simply pointing out that which has actually occurred in the course of human history and illuminating some rather large and irrefutable facts upon which I know we can agree, so that I can then extend the argument from the macrocosm to the microcosm, each of which is the mirror image of the other.

The only reason to look into the past is to learn the lessons that history so richly affords in order to apply those lessons to our lives today, thus allowing us to avoid the same ugly pitfalls and enjoy significantly more freedom. Let us therefore look at another kind of dynamic that the 20/20 vision of hindsight can show us. Let us look at some examples where one person's decision to wage peace literally changed the world.

Mohandas Gandhi was a man who, at the pinnacle of his influence in India, did not own any property, not even the clothes on his back. He saw what he perceived to be a massive injustice perpetrated by the British colonial rulers on the people of India and sought to change it by a very different method than that which had been more commonly employed in the annals of human civilization. He lived and advocated change through peaceful, non-violent means. The British could beat him, which they most assuredly did, and they could put him in jail, which they also did, but Gandhi refused to respond violently to violence. He refused to advocate injustice as a way to fight injustice. He did not seek revenge against the British. He simply wanted them to leave the affairs of the Indian people to the Indian people, and he sought to do so using the only weapon he had at his disposal. Peace. He found something not unlike that which Viktor Frankl found in the in the Nazi concentration camps: no matter what someone else does or says to me, they cannot touch that which lives inside me, unless I allow it.

There is nothing more powerful than an idea whose time has come.

Chapter Three - The Illusion Of Control

Gandhi understood that the idea of peace in the heart of one man is more powerful than any army that has ever been created by the hand of man. The combined strength of the mighty British Empire was entirely powerless in comparison to the idea of peace that lived in his heart because the idea of peace lives in the heart of every man. *It is the heart of every man.* It touches everyone because it is everyone. The idea of peace is based on the love from which we were all created. This love is of God. That which is of God is beyond the ability of man to change or destroy. But it is well within our ability to accept, nurture, and allow to grow and blossom.

Martin Luther King, Jr. was a relatively young African American man, just barely out of his doctoral program at Boston University, the ink of his dissertation not yet dry, when circumstance, or what might otherwise be called the hand of God, propelled him to the forefront of the American Negro's struggle to end institutionalized segregation and to gain the same civil rights that were enjoyed by white Americans. He demanded that black Americans be allowed to enjoy the same rights that were called "inalienable" in the Declaration of Independence written by Thomas Jefferson 200 years before. These rights had been legally and systematically denied people of color, and it was time for all of that to change.

His leadership in the non-violent boycott of the Montgomery Bus service that followed the imprisonment of Rosa Parks when she refused to give up her seat on the bus to a white man was a monumental success. Over the course of his very short career as a civil rights leader, a career that was prematurely ended by a bullet from an assassin's rifle, King discovered that non-violent and peaceful resistance was eminently more powerful than advocating full-scale and violent revolution. He understood that violence begets violence, that war has only ever succeeded in sowing the seeds of the next war, and that the rights his people so richly deserved could not be won at the expense of any of the rights enjoyed by white people. He learned that it was ultimately in the best interest of all Americans, no matter to which race or religion they belonged, to have people living and working together in an atmosphere of mutual respect and peace. He instinctively understood that nobody wins unless everybody wins and that it is impossible for anyone to lose in an atmosphere of peace. It was to this end that King dedicated his life.

Martin Luther King, Jr, was beaten; his house was bombed on more than one occasion; he was repeatedly thrown into exceedingly small jail cells and made to defend himself against some rather creative and mostly absurd trumped-up charges. He also managed to place himself on the receiving end of a massive campaign of attempted control and interdiction waged by none other than the formidable J. Edgar Hoover and the FBI. He steadfastly refused to respond in kind. His message of peaceful, non-violent resistance gained a foothold and kept growing because the idea of peace and the idea of love is who we really are and, try as we might, we cannot separate ourselves from our source. We are all created as an extension of God, who is only love. When we allow the idea of peace or love to enter our conscious mind, we are completing a connection to our Real Source, which has always existed but has been largely forgotten. Making this connection is a little like plugging a light into a wall socket and finally being able to view the most magnificent and enchanting room your imagination could conceive. Once exposed to such a place, you never want to leave it again.

King's attitude of non-violence, the belief in attaining legal equality with white Americans through peaceful means rather

Chapter Three - The Illusion Of Control

than the time-honored eye-for-an-eye and tooth-for-a-tooth mentality that would only insure he had lowered himself to incorporating the very same methods he believed to be unjust, his pervasive belief that the peaceful position was the most powerful one, could not be touched because it is eternal. It is based on truths that cannot be changed, altered, or destroyed by man, because these truths are not of man. They are of God.

Jesus Christ was a man whose ministry lasted only three years at a time and in a place that certainly lacked all of the modern means of communication that exist today. No computers, faxes, modems, cell phones, satellite hook-ups, or internet connections existed. He obviously lacked the means to instantaneously broadcast his message to audiences all around the world that many "world leaders" have at their disposal today. He personally interacted with and reached fewer people in his entire life than Jerry Falwell or Pat Robinson do in one hour on a Sunday morning television show. He also made a whole lot less money than the misters Falwell and Robertson do.

Christ's simple message of love transformed the world. Yet the message of folks like Robertson and Falwell enjoy only a very limited appeal. I wonder why. Could it be that they are not based on the same eternal truths of love, forgiveness, and peace that Christ, Gandhi, and King lived and preached? Can I hear an "Amen"?

Jesus preached a message of love and forgiveness. He taught that it is best to live and let live, to love your neighbor as yourself. He did not place any asterisks or caveats after his message. He did not say, "Let he who is without sin cast the first stone, unless, of course, the person you happen to be stoning is Muslim if you are Christian, Serb if you are a Croat, Tutsi if you are a Hutu, black if you are white, Palestinian if you are an Israeli, or vice versa." No, the love that he preached was a universal love, one that works for everybody, everywhere, any time it is chosen. His message was simple and profound, and the important thing was that he lived the message. He walked the talk rather than just talking the talk. And his message was so powerful that it changed the world. The sum total of all the havoc and destruction that mankind has wreaked upon itself since the beginning of time is **nothing** compared to the absolute healing power of Christ's simple message.

That which is of man cannot live, while that which is of God is all that lives.

Jesus, like Frankl, Gandhi, and King after him, understood that there is not a force on the face of the planet that is strong enough to remotely touch that which is based on love. He instinctively knew that happiness, contentment, peace, joy, and love were to be found inside because that happens to be the place where we connect to our source, which is God. No earthly power could ever remove, alter, or in any way adversely affect our connection to God because this connection is who we really are. It is our very nature, the source of all that is real, the wellspring of our true strength. "Father, forgive them for they know not what they do" is the embodiment of the power and veracity of this eternal truth.

Think about it. Over time, the legacies of people like Genghis Khan, Joseph Stalin, and Adolf Hitler, fade and crumble into the dust of non-existence from which they were originally created. Conversely, the legacies of people like Martin Luther King, Jr., Mohandas Gandhi, Jesus Christ, Mother Theresa, Krishna, and Buddha live forever and can be found in a million different places. A message of love is eternal; it transcends

Chapter Three - The Illusion Of Control

time and never fades. Our only job in life is to consciously choose love, choose to connect to our source, and everything else will literally take care of itself.

Given the choice – and you really do have the choice – wouldn't you really rather have eternal power on your side?

Chapter Three - The Illusion Of Control

YOU ARE NOT YOUR EGO

If love is all that is real and the idea of peace is based on love; if this reality has been demonstrated to be the only thing that freely flows across time and unites one generation to the next; if you can begin to understand that the love of God and the idea of peace has always existed inside you and is really who you are; and if you can accept that you have merely forgotten that love is your source, does it not then make perfect sense to get out of the way of this ultimately healing and eternal energy and allow it to point the way for you? Doesn't it make sense to allow God and the thought of God, with the Holy Spirit as your Guide, to direct your life for you rather than constantly struggling to make things work out from an entirely limited human point of view? Don't you think it would be a whole lot easier to live a life of peace rather than deciding to struggle with all there seems to be to struggle with every day? Especially if being able to do so requires nothing more of you than a willingness to change your mind about yourself, which, after all, is exactly what you have always wanted to do.

You have the ability to choose peace, joy, happiness, serenity, and love, any time you want, and it doesn't cost you a dime. You simply need to remember who you really are and allow Him to direct the show.

Choose peace and you never have to be concerned about shallow concepts such as control again. You will never have to feel the anxiety that arises when you think your life is not going exactly how you think it should. You will never again have to experience the constant hum of fear, anger, frustration, and intolerance as you live your daily life, because you will instinctively know that everything will work out exactly as it should and in ways that are well beyond your limited human ability to conceive. You will clearly know that God can and will do for you what you cannot do for yourself.

So how can you apply the macrocosmic lessons of history to the everyday situations that manifest themselves in your life? Remember, the dynamics which govern the relationships between nations, religions, and races are the exact same as those which play out on a smaller-scale, interpersonal level. Bear in mind that it is *people* who make decisions to build concentration camps. It is *people* who decide that one country needs to invade and subjugate the people of another nation for the good of all concerned. It is *people* who decide that their religion is the one true faith and all others are abominations in the eyes of God. It is *people* who decide that a little bit of ethnic cleansing would be a good idea in order to achieve a position of superiority or because the illusion of superiority already exists. And **fear** is always the basis of such decisions.

People who make decisions on an international level are subject to, and driven by, the exact same fear that drives a man to beat his wife in order to maintain his version of control. It is the exact same fear that tells a parent it is a good thing to beat a child "for his own good" and to tell that child, "This will hurt me more than it hurts you." It is the exact same fear that drives an employer to sexually harass an employee. It is the exact same fear that motivates people in the office to gossip about other people. It is the exact same fear that prompts a kid who does not get his own way in the ball game to take his ball and go home so nobody can play. And it is the exact same fear that drives an alcoholic to take that next drink.

A Course In Miracles tells us that there are no degrees of difficulty in miracles which is the same as saying that there are no degrees of wrong in error. Error is error is error. So whether

Chapter Three - The Illusion Of Control

you are building a concentration camp, starting a war, beating your wife, selling drugs at the local schoolyard, or berating another human being in a hurtful way, it is all the same. The *Course* also teaches that we really only get to choose between love and fear, between truth and illusion. The real power that any individual has is the power to make that choice, and not choosing is actually choosing.

Thoughts, feelings, behaviors, and attitudes always fall into one of two categories; They are either expressions of love, or they are a call for love, which is fear. Love and fear cannot co-exist. You are always choosing either one or the other. You are either acting out of love or you are acting out of fear. If you choose love and peace as your guides, you are choosing all that is. If you choose fear, which is decidedly easier to default to in the short term, you are merely accepting illusion and allowing that which has no life to run your life. Choosing life sure makes sense to me. In the immortal words of John Lennon, "Love is all there is."

What do you think would be the impact if an entire nation woke up (literally and figuratively) one fine and glorious morning and decided that, no matter what, peace is the only option?

We can readily see the impact of a thirty-something carpenter who lived over 2,000 years ago. We can feel the reverberations of a thirty-something African American who, armed with nothing more than the truth, was able to bring the ugliness of racism and bigotry to the conscious awareness of so many people. We have witnessed the history making journey of a young Indian man who didn't even own the clothes on his back and was able to transform an entire nation and inspire so many to look inside to find their real strength. Yet these are examples of individual human beings, individual people with the courage and determination to walk a different path. Can you imagine the altogether indescribably magnificent worldwide changes that would immediately take place if an entire nation collectively decided that no matter what, it would only wage peace? Wow!

If immensely powerful armies and nations cannot change that which lives in the heart and mind of a single individual, neither can you. You do not have the control, you only think you do. Actually, you probably haven't even thought much about it, and you are just operating on automatic pilot, never stopping to take the time to discover where your attitudes come from or to question why you think in certain ways. You probably don't even feel the need to question your thinking unless there happens to be some sort of crisis or situation involving another person causing a wee bit of angst in your life. Whereupon you most definitely default to the file in which you immediately question the other person's thinking and set about the task of straightening *him* out. This never occurs unless the other person agrees to change his thinking or behavior, the appropriateness of which is his decision to make much the same as your attitudes, thoughts, feelings, and behaviors are *always your choice* and are never foisted upon you nor dictated to you by anyone else.

I remember a time that I was traveling to a Club Med. I think that on this particular occasion I was at the club in Cancun, back in the days when I was much younger and a whole lot crazier. Club Med was a great vacation for me because I felt entirely comfortable going alone, secure in the knowledge that I would find other people to hang out with for the week and begin some new friendships. I also felt a certain sense of security in the understanding that any friendships I developed

Chapter Three - The Illusion Of Control

would be of the long-distance sort and would not require much time and attention on my part nor scrutiny on theirs.

I loved the water sports and didn't spend much time laying in the sun working on a world-class tan. I met a woman from New York City (I think everybody that goes to Club Med is from New York City, and we ignited a rather intense evening together. Our paths didn't cross again until the following evening because I had been off doing a day's worth of water sports, which I previously mentioned was great fun for me. And besides, I wasn't running around looking for her all day because I knew that I would most likely see her again at dinner. I had places to go and things to do. When finally we did meet, she was acting rather peculiarly and I asked her what was on her mind. She told me that she did not know how much room to give me. I informed her, in a surprisingly non-indignant and mostly gentle manner, that my room was not hers to give. Needless to say, that romance flamed out faster than a meteor entering earth's atmosphere.

If you can get to a place where you can begin to grasp the concept that no nation in the history of mankind has ever been able to successfully subjugate the people of either their own country or that of another nation, then you can successfully extrapolate that it is impossible for you to successfully dictate the thoughts, feelings, attitudes, or behaviors of anyone else. Sure, you can attain what may seem, in the short run, to be victories. But all you have really succeeded in doing is that which every war that has ever been fought has succeeded in accomplishing: sowing the seeds of the next inevitable confrontation. Remember, the only way to ensure that anyone wins is to insure that everyone wins.

But you may ask, what if someone else does something that

really pisses me off? What if someone knows how to push my buttons; aren't they exercising control over my thoughts and feelings, which then makes everything you wrote pure malarkey? The answer is a firm and resounding **NO.** The fact is that if someone is able to push your buttons, then you have allowed them to do so. Unbeknownst to you, you freely showed them exactly where the button lives and provided them with a remarkably clear and concise set of directions as to exactly how to push it - because you perceive that you can then make them guilty and exercise control over them, in a backwards sort of manner.

Nobody can make you angry without your permission. It is your decision to be angry, scared, or upset about anything that occurs in your life. I am absolutely certain that your ego does not want to hear this because the ego thrives on fostering guilt in you and everybody you can possibly shower guilt upon. It is bad news because it means that you then have to take responsibility for all of your thoughts, feelings, attitudes, and actions - good and bad. And you must constantly be your own monitor, continuously searching inside for the real behavioral motivations that lie just beneath the level of the stories you tell yourself. At first, this is a boatload of work and causes much discomfort. But you eventually learn that looking at yourself as the source of whatever discomfort you feel is the only way to a path of permanent healing and ultimate peace.

If we extend this line of thinking to its next logical level, you can begin to understand that every time somebody else points the accusing finger at you and blathers on about how bad or angry you made them feel you made them feel, you will know it had nothing to do with you and there is nothing to feel guilty about. If your anger or fear is your choice, then everyone else's anger or fear is their choice. Soon the mountain of guilt

Chapter Three - The Illusion Of Control

you have carried around for lo these many years begins to erode and you can walk with more of a spring in your step because that enormous weight is diminishing as fast as you want it to.

The fact of the matter is that nobody else has control over you in any way, shape, or form. You only *think* they do. You have in turn no control over anybody else; you only think you do. Such thinking is purely erroneous and absolutely cannot stand up to honest examination and scrutiny. If you have the courage to honestly examine your own thinking and behavior, you cannot help but arrive at the fact that control is an illusion. It is a lie your ego will keep telling you is a possibility, like a bucket of oats hung just a few inches in front of a starving horse to keep it pulling the wagon.

The ego simply wants you to keep moving in the direction it has determined. It is invested only in keeping enough dust, smoke, and unsettlement in the air to keep you from finding your real direction. The ego wants you to believe the storm is real, that the un-settlement and turmoil you feel every day is all that exists. It wants you to be blinded by the dust cloud so that you will never find the peace that always exists at the center of every storm. Your ego will always seek to convince you that the latest drama is where your attention should be focused so that you will never stop and think that maybe, just maybe, there is another way to go about all of this.

For as long as homo sapiens have walked the surface of this planet, ego has run roughshod over the entire species. Ego tells you that you are extraordinarily important and you are separate from every other human being. Ego says you are alive right now, but when you die you will be gone forever and the world you perceive with your five senses is the real deal

193

while nothing else exists. Ego convinces you that you live in a dog-eat-dog world and you had better start chomping right now if you want to get your fair share. Ego will have you believe if you aren't winning you are losing and if you really want to be a winner, you had better make sure that someone else loses because they are all seeking to make you the loser. And ego will also tell you that whatever you need to do for your survival is absolutely correct.

The ego sets itself up as the guardian of the host. It tells you it is there to take care of you because you really are not able to fend for yourself in such a hostile environment. Ego makes you think that you lack certain tools of the trade necessary to live in the world, but that's ok because the ego has all the tools and will always protect you. The ego sincerely believes in separation and will always come from a place of me-versus-them. The ego will always seek to protect itself, first and foremost, and will fight with the ferocity of a cornered tiger to keep you from acquiring the knowledge that everything it tells you is false. The ego will absolutely sabotage and derail any efforts you make on your own behalf to make alternative choices, because as you became increasingly aware of the truth, the ego will experience its own demise.

Chapter Three - The Illusion Of Control

THAT WHICH YOU CAN CONTROL

The extent to which you buy the lie of the possibility of control and pursue this illusion as though it is real, is the extent to which you will feel guilt in your life and seek to make other people feel guilt. It is an excellent and time-tested formula for engendering feelings of frustration, hatred, anger, intolerance, fear, anxiety, panic, sadness, turmoil, and pain. All of which *is* within your power to eliminate because the one thing you do have control over is whatever you decide.

Underneath the level of your conscious mind lies the level of the decision maker. The job of the ego is to keep you so discombobulated inside the multitudinous dramas of your everyday life that you neglect to remember that the decision maker actually does exist and that an entire world of different decisions and choices are available to you. Decisions and choices that, once made, can immediately free you from the bondage of the extremely limited menu of choices offered by the ego.

You absolutely do have the power to make decisions and choices that will bring more and more peace, joy, love, serenity, and fun into your life every day. You can make decisions and choices that will dramatically diminish the power over you and your life that an ego hell bent on having its own way is currently wielding.

Once you understand and accept that the only real decision you can make is between love and fear and that the decision maker will always correctly make the loving choice for you, you will begin to regain your real power, and the ego's power over you will begin to fade forever.

The ego represents the choice for fear, which manifests itself as confusion, despair, anger, rage, frustration, broken relationships, emotional suffering, isolation, and sadness. Spirit, your Real Self, represents the choice for love, which manifests itself as happiness, peaceful feelings, and a knowing that no matter what appears to be going on in your life, it has been invited by you for your learning pleasure and will only serve to make you stronger and wiser.

As far as the concept of control is concerned, and a concept is all it really is, let's take a look at some things we can all agree are absolutely outside the range of our control or influence. Nobody in his or her right mind really thinks they have control over the weather. I remember, back in August of 1992, Elaine and I were married on a boat in Boston Harbor. The *Lady Christine* was a private yacht we chartered for the wedding and it was just large enough for us to invite around 100 guests for what turned out to be an enormously entertaining evening. Given my druthers, I would have chosen a gloriously warm and sunny mid-August day that evolved into a splendidly clear and mild evening. But the rain began early in the morning and never stopped until we had long since gone to sleep for the night And nobody seemed to notice.

We went to Florida for two weeks after the wedding and had a great time relaxing away from the hustle and bustle of everyday life. We spent the second week on Marco Island until we were rudely jolted out of the pleasant little cocoon we had fashioned for ourselves by the imminent arrival of Hurricane Andrew, the most powerful and savage hurricane ever to slam into the Florida peninsula. The evacuation orders came on a Tuesday, just three days after we arrived, and the week that we had set aside to do nothing but rest and relax was cut dramatically short.

Chapter Three - The Illusion Of Control

Now we had a choice to make. We could spend our time bitterly complaining about the fact that somebody was rude enough to drop such a fierce and menacing hurricane on us. We could have gone so far as to think that the hurricane, as well as the rain on the day of the wedding, materialized with the specific intent of ruining the good time we had planned. We could have been greatly saddened that our married life was starting out under such adverse circumstances and then projected that forward to wonder if the rest of our lives together were going to be visited by one disaster after another.

Instead, we chose to make the most of our situation and gladly joined the endlessly long procession of people clogging the roads leading north. We chose to see ourselves as part of a slowly moving, miles-long party instead of the newly married couple who had been so horribly put upon. We knew we would have a great story to tell when we finally arrived back in the Boston area, and we were fortunate enough to secure what had to be the last room available in Orlando, far enough north so that we were safely out of the path of the oncoming storm. We looked forward to experiencing whatever spontaneous adventures awaited us and seemed to enjoy every minute of the world's longest traffic jam. I can tell you that our attitude was not shared by everyone we encountered on our long journey north.

No, you cannot successfully control the weather. You cannot make the sun shine whenever you would like and the tides rise and fall according to your whim. Nor would you even consider wasting your time in such obviously futile pursuits unless you happen to be either completely off your rocker or playing the role of a mad scientist in a Disney movie, because you intrinsically know it is impossible. Remember, the macro system is exactly the same as the micro system. If you cannot control

197

the larger, more universal picture, you cannot control the smaller, more personal picture. It all works the same way. If you were absolutely clear about the impossibility of being able to control other people, places, and things in the same manner as you are absolutely clear about your inability to manipulate the path of the earth around the sun, you would not even try. And the peace you would feel would grow in direct proportion to your willingness to let go of the illusion of control.

Now, lets take a look at the best-case scenario, where you magically acquire the power you need to successfully control your life by being able to know exactly what the best thing is for you and everyone else you know. In one wave of a magnificent magic wand, you have been given The Big Picture, and you absolutely have the ability to produce and direct the action in ways you think ought to happen. You take out your thousand-pound Daytimer, and everything you plan on goes exactly according to how you think it should; everybody and everything lines up exactly according to how you think things should go. The world and everyone in it are at your service, so to speak. You have become the ultimate orchestra director, skillfully weaving and interweaving the intricate patterns, voices, and dynamic forces that are constantly shifting and changing key. And you are in charge of exactly when and to what extent the shifts and key changes occur and what instruments are engaged in the action.

Your life would be painfully boring. What would you or could you learn? Where would your growth come from? Your life would be characterized by a total absence of excitement, spirit of investigation, risk, chance, spontaneity, and feelings of triumph and challenge. Your existence would be like living in a deep and thick fog where all the colors are a variation on a shade of battleship gray, where the most exciting sound would

Chapter Three - The Illusion Of Control

be the peeling of a distant bell marking the places you need to avoid, lest you run aground in territory that is not part of the finely constructed roadmap of your life. There would be no valleys to show you the hills, and there would be no majestic hills to show you the lush green and fertile valleys. The excitement of the unknown and the wonder of discovery would be gone forever, replaced by the low hum of an idling engine, going nowhere. It would be like taking a finely tuned, eight-cylinder, turbo-charged, super high-performance engine that can accelerate from zero to sixty in four seconds flat and never once applying a single foot-pound of pressure to the accelerator.

The choice, as always, is yours. Go for the control and live a life that is significantly more limited than that which would otherwise be possible. Or let go and enter a world which is more exciting and fulfilling than you can possibly hope to imagine. You cannot have it both ways.

The fact of the matter is that you *are* that finely tuned, eight-cylinder, turbo-charged, super high-performance engine, and you just have to (you must because you are wired that way) stamp your foot down on the gas pedal and hold on for dear life because you really need to see what that engine is capable of doing. And the best thing to do is to use the kind of fuel which is exactly right for the magnificent machine you really are and connect to the True Source of energy and light that assures trouble-free performance. Connect yourself to the pump of the Power that created it all and let go. Then watch your life evolve in ways that are exactly right for you. Satisfaction guaranteed, or your money back.

In order for anyone to attempt to mold other people, places, or things into the expression of what he thinks they *ought* to be, he must first point a finger at them and say they are wrong. This is most likely a very figurative finger, although it really would be a riot to see people walking around on crowded city streets with their arms outstretched and an accusing finger protruding from the end like some sort of error-discovering divining rod. Finger pointing, finding fault in anyone or anything else is playing by the rules of the ego because it establishes an immediate separation. It seeks to lend validity to the erroneous concept of me versus them. It is a way to keep oneself isolated and feeling alone. It is an excellently devised scheme of divide and conquer perpetrated by the ego for the specific purpose of exercising control over you. The ultimate goal in finding fault, error, or wrong wherever that fault, error, or wrong is perceived to be, is to tell yourself that you are the one without the fault, that you are not the one who has made the error, that you are the one who is right. And the only way to do this is through the ego-driven process of separation and isolation.

The problem is that you are trying to do the right thing for the wrong reason, which is a game that is ultimately rigged to produce no winners. You are trying to make yourself feel better about yourself and the world in which you live, but the method you are employing can only end up producing the exact opposite effect: You feel worse. This is a classic example of the cure being worse than the disease.

The answer is to understand and accept that there is nothing wrong with you to begin with, never has been and never will be. So there is no need to make yourself right by making other people wrong. You were created by a loving Force to be the perfect expression of Itself. This is your birthright. It is your Real Self. Your value is intrinsic and derives from no external source. You are as much a part of your Source as your Source is a part of you. Therefore, measuring yourself in any way, shape, or form against anything external is an exercise in futility. You came into the world as an expression of ultimate perfection and peace - and your only job here is to remember that.

Let go and let God.

It works.

CHAPTER FOUR

THE OUTSIDE REFLECTS THE INSIDE

HOW TO ENJOY PEACE IN YOUR LIFE EVERY DAY

Chapter Four - The Outside Reflects The Inside

"If you are distressed by anything external, the pain is not due to the thing itself, but to your estimate of it; And this you have the power to revoke at any moment."

- Marcus Aurelius
(121 - 180 A.D.)

"Seek not to change the world. Seek instead to change your mind about the world."

- A Course In Miracles

"Life does not consist mainly, or even largely, of facts and happenings. It consists mainly of the storm of thought that is forever flowing through one's head."

- Mark Twain

"My religion consists of a humble admiration of the illimitable superior spirit who reveals himself in the slight details we are able to perceive with our frail and feeble minds."

- Albert Einstein

"It is one of the beautiful compensations of this life that no one can sincerely try to help another without helping himself."

- Ralph Waldo Emerson

Chapter Four - The Outside Reflects The Inside

THE BABY KILLER

Hatred, outrage, and abject hostility seized my heart and squeezed it with the savage fury and relentless pressure of a junkyard automobile-crushing machine. I felt like strands of rusty and corroded barbed wire were suddenly and violently pushed through my veins instead of the oxygen-carrying and life-sustaining blood that usually flows through those tiny hollow tubes. I spluttered and spit as the boiling rage that suddenly consumed my body forced my breath to come in short, frantic gasps.

"He's a baby killer! The son of a bitch is a baby killer! Goddamn! Goddamn! Goddamn! The son of a bitch is a baby killer!" are the thoughts that went screaming through my head from a source that was not foreign to me but was nonetheless entirely unwelcome. Yet I could neither stop nor slow the cadence at which these poisonous words reverberated through my head like echoes off deep canyon walls.

I was in the middle of yet another classic battle between my heart and my head. Its eruption was very sudden, very violent, and caught me completely by surprise. Today I know that the kindling for such a reaction was sitting there inside me, without me knowing it was there, just waiting for the right set of circumstances or just the right stimulus to ignite the fire. Unfortunately, I did not yet have enough experience connecting to my heart, and my foundation in congruent thinking (where the head, heart, and the spirit are all in accord) was still sufficiently underdeveloped so this was a fight my head was winning, hands down.

I couldn't get rid of this crazy thought that seemed to inhabit me more than be thought by me. Like an alien predator invading your being and you are powerless to stop it. What in the name of God am I going to do now, I thought, and how in the hell did I ever get mixed up with a guy like that? Christ almighty, the guy is a baby killer, and I picked him to be my sponsor. I actually liked him and admired him. What does that say about me? I can't believe it. What the hell am I going to do now? Panic.

As these horrible thoughts rocketed through my head at the speed of light and filled my heart with a deadly poison, that was far beyond the realm of mere indignation, my left hand plied a vice grip on the steering wheel so tightly that my knuckles turned white. The pain from the grip shot up from my fingers, through my elbow, and blasted into my heretofore unsuspecting and very tender shoulder. With my free right hand, I slammed the car phone back into its receiver with such a savage force that it should have immediately exploded into a million different pieces. I was very disappointed that it actually remained intact. After all, what fun is it to get so worked up and not be able to see some tangible outside physical destruction to complement the meltdown occurring on the inside?

I was driving on route 495 and the night was so dark it was as if the entire interstate highway had been completely covered by an impenetrable black shroud that eradicated whatever stray pieces of light might otherwise have been available. The darkness was entirely appropriate because it exactly matched the monstrous lack of light that had so suddenly invaded my highly susceptible being. The lack of light was so severe that it reminded me of those times when, as a sensitive young boy, I would pull the covers up over my head to create an imaginary cave for purposes of hiding out in whatever fantasy game happened to be running through my mind at the time. But this

Chapter Four - The Outside Reflects The Inside

night was remarkably lacking in the delicious feelings of safety and protection that emanated from the deeper recesses of my soul as I played out my imaginary adventures in the relative safety of my childhood bed.

Paul was the unfortunate subject of the sudden flow of invective that my brain, once having latched onto something so explosive, fought to hang on to with the determination of a Pit Bull Terrier protecting a hunk of raw meat. Of course, Paul had no idea that I had erupted into such a frenzy over the conversation we just had, which is not much of a surprise. He had no idea that something he said touched off an internal firestorm that rivaled the destruction of Dresden. Paul was sitting comfortably in his warm and cozy home, peacefully believing that he had just shared a painful part of his story with a guy he sponsors. He further believed that he was being helpful to me. As it turned out, he may well have saved my life, but I was nowhere near thinking so at the time. Yes, God does work in mysterious ways, His wonders to perform.

While I was in the middle of this latest storm of runaway irrational thinking, I sincerely believed the horrible thoughts I was experiencing, which had so rudely intruded on my life, had only to do with Paul. I was wrong. They had to do with me. So I tooled along, driving faster and faster, steeped in the boil of my own unquenchable fury.

There I was, driving at an increasing rate of speed and in a blind rage on a dark and forbidding highway, shaking and vibrating to the tunes of the emotional tremors that were pulsating through my now jacked-up system, screaming and cursing into the solitary night without the satisfaction of having another human ear available to receive the volcano of poison spouting from my lips and to become as infected as I was.

Misery does love company. And Paul was relaxed and at peace in the warmth and comfort of his own family room while I, exploding and enraged, screamed along at ungodly rates of speed. It hardly seemed fair.

Paul was my sponsor in Alcoholics Anonymous, and sponsorship in AA is another of those strokes of pure genius that has convinced me, beyond any doubt whatsoever, that the entire program has been Divinely inspired. Based on the time-honored spiritual premise that the best way to grow and expand the love that most assuredly lives inside us is to give it away, the idea of sponsorship is the embodiment of the notion that the best way to stay sober is to help others gain their sobriety. You can't keep it unless you give it away, as the saying goes.

This is how it works. When people first summon the courage to show their weary faces at an AA meeting, they have usually reached some level of physical, mental, or spiritual bankruptcy. More often than not, it is all three. AA is usually considered the last stop. It is fairly common for newcomers to be reeling from lives filled with fear, anger, suspicion, and isolation. It is also not a huge stretch of the imagination to understand that they could definitely use some very personal assistance to help them through the difficulties of getting sober and trying to successfully live in the world from which they spent so long seeking escape through the abuse of alcohol and other drugs.

Newcomers are a mess, and they need to have their hands held by those who have been there, done that. Also, they have just come off a life of successfully pulling their particular brand of denial on themselves and sheer bullshit on most other people, including their very own families, bosses, and co-workers.

Therefore, it is important for a newcomer to interact with someone on a regular basis who is not going to buy their lies and excuses and will tell them exactly what to do.

Chapter Four - The Outside Reflects The Inside

MAKING THE CHANGE PERMANENT

Before I go too far into this chapter, I want to clarify something that may be of importance to you. This book is not about how someone who becomes an alcoholic can recover from a deadly disease and live a rich and rewarding life. It is about how ANYBODY can recover from the dis-ease of life and learn to enjoy a level of joy, peace, serenity, and grace that otherwise would be denied to them. This book is for anybody who wants to grow into the person God originally intended them to be. My goal is to point out that the only one keeping you trapped in whatever rut you have fallen into, whether or not you are aware of the rut, looks back at you from the mirror every day.

The only way to successfully and permanently change your life is to understand that the decision to make the change and the commitment to see the evolution through to its magnificent conclusion, are squarely within your power. It is also my opinion that the only way to ensure permanent and lasting success is to learn how to change the way you think. You need to learn to interpret the world and everything in it according to a different set of rules. It is your perspective and the underlying assumptions that must change, nothing else. Change these, and you will be amazed how different the world looks.

It is impossible to make a permanent change, one that you can count on day in and day out, through thick and thin, unless you consciously make a shift in your internal dynamic. In order for you to make the necessary shift, you must first examine your own thinking. You must look at the places you get stuck as being caused by you and nobody or anything else. You must change the default setting in your internal computer, but you cannot do so until you know the default setting exists. My goal is to convince you of the existence of the default setting as the vital first step in adjusting the setting.

The best way I can think of to show you to yourself is to show me to you. This can work because we are all very much alike and function according to the same principles. We may look different on the outside and our life's situations may bear no resemblance, one to the other. However, we are but variations on a theme, and we are all irrevocably connected on the inside. My goal is to teach you, through a series of personal stories, that you have the power to change your life by changing your thinking.

In order to do so, you must first look at your own thinking as the source of your discomfort. It is through my stories that I hope to show you where I was stuck, the pain it caused me and others, and how I worked myself out of my own way. I truly believe that the change I made is not only permanent but will continue to evolve and get better because I have learned to look at my own thinking as the source of any problems I have. This process works whether or not you have slid down the slope into active addiction, whatever the drug of choice may be. The only difference between someone who becomes an alcoholic and someone who does not is the drug-addicted person takes hiding from who he or she really is to a different level.

The vast majority of the people in the world do not know they have the power to make the changes they wish because they do not see themselves as the cause of the pain. Also, most people do not wish to see the truth because it can make them decidedly uncomfortable. It is much too easy to succumb to the allure of the familiar. Dying to the old in order to live to the new takes enormous courage and faith. It has been well

Chapter Four - The Outside Reflects The Inside

said that a man who conquers a city is nothing compared to a man who conquers himself. Where do you come down?

This is not kind of self-help book that will give you ten simple steps to the secret of happiness. Simply changing behavior according to some magic formula given to you in a series of repeatable steps will not work. It will not work for the same reason diets of one kind or another do not work. It is a proven fact that most people who go on a diet to lose weight end up putting more weight back on than they lost. This is because simply changing behavior does not necessarily change the internal hard drive. However, challenging your thinking and changing your thought process will lead to the permanent change you seek.

In this chapter, I will teach you something that can change your life, and I will illustrate it by way of my own experience. You will learn that what you see occurring on the outside is an accurate reflection of that which is occurring on the inside. The message is that if you want to change your experience of the world, make the internal change first, and the outside world will take care of itself. I found this when I discovered that anything I accused anyone else of in my thinking, I really thought about myself. It is so true: whenever you find yourself pointing an accusing finger at someone else, there are three fingers pointing back at you.

I found this truth as a result of the reaction I experienced to the story Paul related to me. I will get to how it all went together, but first a little background.

Chapter Four - The Outside Reflects The Inside

I THINK I AM GOING TO LIVE

The story of how I met my sponsor is yet another in the never-ending series of joyful "coincidences" telling me, most convincingly, that God is always doing for me that which I cannot do for myself. So, if you don't mind, I will digress just a little bit in order to relay the story because it occupies an important place in my life's larger mosaic. I also wish to tell it because this story accurately reflects nearly all the principles I am trying to convey in this book. It is the microcosm that contains the macrocosm. It will help you understand how I was able to get from there to here, and it will help illuminate more than one exceedingly important lesson in how to attain real peace in your life.

I need to take you back to when I was the sole occupant of a beautiful 10-room Victorian home in very urban Dorchester (part of the City of Boston) and how one remark I made to my erstwhile therapeutic tag team led me, through a series of amazing "coincidences," to living alone in a nine-room contemporary in very rural Stow.

Dorchester is considered by many to be the inner city. By contrast, I think there are more cows in Stow than there are people. But I found myself living there nonetheless. It was while living in Stow that I finally found my way into the program of Alcoholics Anonymous, put a long overdue end to the dry drunk phase of my life, and subsequently met my AA sponsor.

As the story unfolds, you will begin to notice that this is yet another in the long list of scripts that I could never have written for myself. As creative an individual as I am today, back then I considered myself highly fortunate if I simply made it through the day without causing myself or anybody else serious bodily harm. I will offer unmistakable evidence of how the Hand of God has always been working in my life without my being aware of it right away. I will ask you to take a good hard look at some of the things that have occurred in your life, often without any advance planning on your part, and notice how one apparently isolated and relatively unimportant event could not have happened unless a similarly isolated and unimportant event had already occurred.

I will then ask you to take the leap and notice how you could not possibly be where you are today without having experienced a string of these unrelated and seemingly insignificant events. I will ask you to take a dispassionate and objective a look a your own life so you can see that God has been working the same magic in your life, weaving the fabric of these isolated events into the mosaic that has become your destiny - a destiny you could never have planned all by yourself, one that has brought you to this page in this book for a reason.

If you look for it, you will find it. And if you keep looking, you will see it everywhere. This realization will bring untold levels of peace, joy, happiness, excitement, and hope, to your daily life because it will tell you that you are much better off not being in charge of the details. You will also find that you cannot help but reach the most logical conclusion of all, which is that no matter how bleak things look to you or how miserable you have become on the inside, you will be carried and well taken care of, because that is precisely what has already occurred. The entire game of life is wired in your favor. At one point in my life, and the point was over six years long, I was the bleakest and most miserable son of a bitch on the face of the planet. Yet I was carried to exactly the place and in exactly the way I needed to be without having the slightest clue that it was happening. And there is no difference between you

Chapter Four - The Outside Reflects The Inside

and me. You are already being quite taken care of, whether you know it or not.

Take a look at your life from the perspective I just outlined and you can't help but see that what I am saying is true. If you sincerely come to believe you have indeed been carried to this point, then you can make the leap to understanding you will be carried the rest of the way as well. What a relief! You can actually let go of the future and rid yourself of any fearful thoughts of the future. Instead, you can be energized and excited because you know right down to the bottom of your soul that your life will be dramatically better than you could ever imagine today.

Dorchester is a very interesting place. Back in the nineteenth century, it was an upper-class suburb of Boston. It was the place to which the people of South Boston and other parts of the growing city moved when they made enough money to buy or build some of the finest homes you can imagine. A thriving Jewish population that had sprung up along Blue Hill Avenue began moving into the nearby town of Milton to avoid the burgeoning white Irish Catholic migration from the city. Probably the most prominent of these movers and shakers to settle into then-rural Dorchester was John "Honey Fitz" Fitzgerald, who later became the Mayor of Boston and was also the father of Rose Fitzgerald, the most famous graduate of Dorchester High School.

Rose lived her life and came of age in the fashionable Boston society and eventually married Joseph P. Kennedy. Rose and Joe actively embraced a long-standing Irish Catholic tradition and became the proud parents of many children, not the least of which was John F. Kennedy. Many of these prominent Bostonians built their stunning and grand Victorian homes in the fashionable Ashmont Hill area. The 10-room home that I owned and in which I was the sole occupant was one of the smaller of these fine houses.

During the sixties and seventies the phenomenon of white flight played itself out in Boston so that Dorchester underwent another transition from totally white Irish Catholic where one's parish was the defining geographical identity, to a virtual partitioning of neighborhoods based entirely upon ethnic heritage, including African American, Vietnamese, and Hispanic. In the early seventies, a highly divisive and fear-filled crisis around court-ordered school desegregation proved to be the gasoline that was thrown onto the fires of ethnic migration so that the Dorchester of today, as well as the one I left in 1989, is a proverbial melting pot of racial and cultural diversity. Modest by comparison, my 10-room Victorian was located on Walton Street in the Ashmont Hill section of the city, one block from where the Fitzgerald mansion stood until it burned down.

One day, as I was driving to work in the morning, I happened to notice a rather stately Georgian mansion that I had curiously never seen before. I drove down this particular street every day for well over a year, and this house had never once registered even a single half of a blip on my radar screen. It was as though the house had simply materialized overnight, and I couldn't remember the other house that had previously occupied this meticulously manicured lot. Scotty, beam it in! This is very odd because the house was one of a kind. It really stood out and virtually demanded that you not only look at it, but that you stop to study such an inspired and incredible design. It was also in remarkable condition for a house that was well over 100 years old.

Isn't it funny how you don't see things until you are ready to

Chapter Four - The Outside Reflects The Inside

see them. I have found that this remarkable human phenomenon occurs for two reasons. The first is that you have become emotionally and spiritually ready to move on to some sort of new and interesting phase in your life. Seeing whatever it is that happens to appear for what would seem to be the very first time is the very experience that serves as the launching pad for this new adventure. The second reason could be that you have already been tooling along on a consciously undertaken journey of self discovery, growth, and learning. Actually seeing something for the very first time that has been there, right in front of you for quite a while, is just another way to confirm in your heart and soul that you are on the right path.

Either way, if you look deeply enough when, at some point in the future you are looking back at how the brickwork of your path in life has been laid down, you can't help but notice the unfathomable and delicate touch of the Hand of God moving you along.

It just so happens that I had been getting very tired of the tedium, and intellectual constriction of the paper business in general, as well as the terrible changes that were taking place in my own company in particular. I just could not grow down to that level anymore, and I needed to find a place where the air was fresh, new, and mine. I must say the paper business had served me well. I was rather fortunate to have landed there in the first place because it had carried me from being a poor college graduate to having some semblance of financial freedom. But the business had gotten pretty old and I was desperately in need of a change. I had begun to think that opening a bed and breakfast would be a good idea and when I saw the big blue Georgian, I knew this was the ideal place. So I mentioned my idea to the previously discussed erstwhile therapeutic tag team and everything went screaming downhill (or uphill depending on your perspective) from there. As it turned out, the tag team was having some rather formidable financial difficulties of their own and, apparently, saw my idea as a way to help them out a little bit.

They talked me out of locating my new business brainchild in the City of Boston, which was really outside their sphere of every day influence. They talked me into seriously looking around the more rural MetroWest area, territory with which they were more familiar. They volunteered to help me find a place, which worked for me because I knew absolutely nothing about MetroWest outside of the fact that there seemed to be more cows and horses than people. This was a foreign country to someone born and raised in the city. Yet I trusted them because I had nobody else left. I had essentially trashed all of my friends and family by this time.

I believe they used the influence they had gained over me to move me along according to their agenda and, no doubt, saw my as-yet-unopened business as a way to help them solve some of their money problems. Somehow, the help they volunteered transmuted into their having a 50% share in the business that I was going to run, and I remained clueless as to exactly how that came about. But everything happens for a reason, and God always has a better plan than that which we could ever dream of devising with our own severely limited human perspective. So the search ended up in a place nobody could have predicted.

The first time I saw the sign, it sent an unmistakable chill through me, and I can still see the sign and feel the wonder of that heart-warming and blood-stirring chill today. "Entering Stow" is what it said, and the emotional charge it created in me reached all the down to the very depths of my soul. It

Chapter Four - The Outside Reflects The Inside

touched something inside me that is not of me. I cannot explain this reaction in any rational manner other than to say God was showing me the path that was right for me. Prior to the spring afternoon when I first saw the sign, I had never been to Stow and I didn't know the first thing about the town. Yet I instantaneously knew, like I know that staying alive depends on the ability to keep breathing, that the town of Stow was where I was going to live.

I abandoned the idea of the bed and breakfast because I had become increasingly uncomfortable with the idea and because it had already served its purpose of showing me the "Entering Stow" sign. I eventually purchased a single-family home on Lowell Drive in Stow and moved into the house in October of 1989.

Moving to Stow was an interesting experience to say the very least. I knew so little about the place that when I was en route to the house I was buying to meet my real estate agent there for a second house tour, I got lost. I promise you that I had no idea where I was. I had to call the house to be guided in like the unwitting and inexperienced non-pilot we see in the movies that takes over the controls after the real pilot suffers a fatal heart attack. I needed to be talked through a safe landing by a handler in the control tower.

I think it is really funny that I literally did not even know where the house was, yet I was buying it, so vital was the feeling that I needed to move to Stow. And moving to Stow was only a part of the strong and inexplicable feelings about my impending move that were going on inside at the time.

You can't imagine the reactions of the people I told about buying a house in Stow. "Where in the hell is Stow?" and "You're buying a house *where*?" were common questions. My decision to live in Stow at the time surprised most of the people I knew because I was such a city rat. I must also say that it surprised me as well because I was really incapable of making such a monumental and life-changing decision, let alone executing it.

Making such a move with all of my mental and emotional faculties firing on all cylinders and an army of close friends for help and support would have been an extremely difficult thing to do. But I was not firing on all cylinders, or even a quarter of my cylinders, and I had no close friends for help and support. While I worked hard to look good on the outside, I was in truth all alone, crumbling, and collapsing on the inside. I was also out-of-my-mind terrified about making this very unlikely and uncharacteristic move, but I made myself keep going when halting the process seemed such a good idea on many occasions. I just knew there was something there for me.

I was in good physical shape because I found that exercise helped to keep me at least temporarily tethered to terra firma. I owned a number of properties and I drove an expensive foreign car. But I eventually learned that none of it was worth the powder to blow itself to hell because I was so miserable and so crazy. I was at the end of a six and a half year dry drunk; I had severed my ties with the erstwhile therapeutic tag team and the "support" they offered just before the actual move; I had alienated everybody in my entire family; I had no close friends to speak of because I was really no fun to hang around with; and I was not involved in an intimate relationship with anyone because I simply lacked the capacity for intimacy.

However, the decision seemed to have been made for me, and I had nothing left to do but go along with it to the best of my ability because some very peculiar things were happening.

Chapter Four - The Outside Reflects The Inside

From somewhere down deep in the interior of my mind, heart, and soul, an image of a white church came to me whenever I thought about my impending move. It came from the same place the words "My God , I'm home" came from during my first AA meeting. It bubbled up into my conscious mind from a place that is much greater than my seriously limited smaller self and for which the small self is totally incapable of conjuring a logical explanation. This image lived in me as though it was sewn to my soul, and I could feel it as though it was a real three-dimensional presence in my chest. I cannot explain this other than to say that, once again, I was being shown what to do. It sometimes completely consumed my entire interior screen, and I knew that there was a white church somewhere in Stow with my name on it. It was enough to keep me going.

One of the truly fascinating things that occurred as a result of purchasing the house and making my move to Stow was that it proved to be the thing that finally put an end to the relationship I had with the erstwhile therapeutic tag team. Indeed, God works in many mysterious ways, His wonders to perform. The last meeting I had with the people who had been so influential in my life, and may well have caused me more harm than good, was one in which I said a couple of rather prophetic things. I told them that I had no idea what was wrong with me. Today I know that one of the biggest problems was that I had been having the life squeezed out of me for a very long while by the very people with whom I was then meeting. But they did not know it any more than I did and I have long since forgiven them. But I told them that I really did know two things: I had to get God into my life somewhere, somehow, some way, and I had no idea how to do go about doing that. And that I needed to tell someone my story, and I did not really know what that meant.

So, there I was, moving to Stow, completely on my own with nobody to talk to and an image of a white church so indelibly imprinted on my interior landscape that it felt like it was actually built into my chest with wood, nails and concrete. The weekend after I moved in, I found a white church, a Unitarian Universalist Church, located right next to Stow's only traffic light. I began to attend Sunday services and even ran into (small world of small worlds) a couple of people I knew from my business life. I took this as a sign that I was in the right place but something about it just did not feel right. I soon discovered that there was another white church just down the road, a non-denominational Christian church, so I decided to do some further investigation.

The following Sunday I arrived at this new church uncharacteristically early. I was somewhat surprised to feel that now familiar glow of excitement stirring around in my heart and soul, a tingling sensation that emanated from the center of my being and radiated out to all extremities, telling me I was in the right place. I walked in and plopped myself down somewhere around the middle and in a place where there wasn't another person so close that they might try to start a conversation with me. One can't be too careful, you know. I had noticed on the sign outside the church that the minister's name was David Dodge. I watched with mounting interest as he walked down the center isle at the beginning of the service. When he turned to face the congregation, not one person of whom I was even remotely familiar, something struck me.

There was a definite incongruity between his eyes and his clerical robes. There was a turmoil, a tension, and a pain in his eyes that simply did not jibe with the symbol of serenity that the robes represented. To say that my interest was piqued would be an understatement, and I determined I was going to

Chapter Four - The Outside Reflects The Inside

hang around that place until I got my answers.

I cannot tell you what the sermon was about that morning nor is it of any importance. But I can tell you that during the sermon David mentioned that he was an alcoholic and that he had been sober in Alcoholics Anonymous for quite some time. This really resonated with me, and I began to understand the distinct polarity and palpable tension between the expression in his eyes and the pastoral serenity of his robes.

Over the next few weeks, I made it a point to attend Sunday services at The Union Church of Stow and I began to meet some very nice people who weren't only interested in getting something from me or trying to determine what I could do for them. I also began to build a relationship of sorts with David Dodge. Having grown up as an inner city Catholic boy, I found this whole experience of attending a protestant church in the middle of cow country to be very exciting and full of promise. Remember, I mentioned to the tag team that I needed to get God in my life somewhere, somehow, some way but that I really did not know how. Well, here I was, sitting right down front, in the very first pew, every Sunday morning, finally walking on a path toward God that I could actually identify, and I had virtually nothing to do with being there. I certainly could not have planned it that way. I was merely following my nose, and it was God who was showing my nose the direction in which to point.

One of those Sunday mornings, about three or four weeks after I began to attend services at the Union Church, I found myself walking to the social hour that always followed the services with none other than David Dodge. We were talking about something and finally broached the subject of his being an alcoholic. I told him that I used to drink a lot but that I stopped drinking on my own. I can still remember the way he looked at me when I shared this bit of personal history with him. He just glanced at me with an extremely loving, thoughtful, knowing, and somewhat mirthful look. He smiled in a such a way as to convey that he already knew a lot more about what was going on with me than I did. The smile also conveyed a hope that someday I would figure out for myself what he already knew.

Chapter Four - The Outside Reflects The Inside

<u>NOPE, LOOKS LIKE I AM GOING TO DIE</u>

A couple of weeks later I was still out of my mind and so consumed by a palpable sense of isolation, fear, and despair, that I could not imagine anything or anyone, including God, ever being able to put an end to my suffering. One inordinately desperate Sunday morning I sat alone in my kitchen, essentially reviewing my options. I was sick and tired of being sick and tired. My desperation had reached an all-time high. I had had quite enough, thank you very much, of being absolutely out of my mind. I just did not want the rage, anger, fear, paranoia, crazy thinking, and stone-cold loneliness anymore. I was done, as done as the day I knew that I could not drink anymore. I had reached the limit. The bottom had finally come.

The way I saw it, I had only two options left. The first one was to go out drinking and picking up women again. Even though I knew at some level that would most assuredly lead to an early grave, at least I could have a little fun along the way. Why not? This sobriety thing was certainly no picnic, and I couldn't identify any good it had accomplished. The other option was to kill myself now and just get it over with. One way or the other, a decision needed to be made right now and there were only two options left, both of which would leave me quite dead, an outcome that seemed to be perfectly acceptable to me.

I sat and brooded over these two very real options for quite some time, alternately weighing the relative merits of each in much the same way as I would decide between pizza or Chinese food. Actually, the occasional battle that raged in my mind between pizza and Chinese were much more emotionally charged than the debate over which method of death I would ultimately choose. Then, out of the clear blue, came a third option.

Chapter Four - The Outside Reflects The Inside

<u>GOD WAS THERE ALL ALONG</u>

I remembered a relationship I had with a woman a few years before. I think I can call it a relationship because we were seeing each other for slightly more than four weeks, which was a record for me in the post-drinking days. As near as I can recall, there was nothing very electric happening between us, but we seemed to get along ok. However, after a few weeks the facade of looking good begins to wear away, exposing the slightly ugly and crumbling reality below. Eventually, she told me that she thought I was an adult child of an alcoholic because I had shared with her some of what it was like growing up with an alcoholic father. She put that together with the often erratic behavior I exhibited, added one plus one, and came up with a right-on-the-money accurate answer of two.

I can picture her in my mind's eye right now and wish I could remember her name because I owe her a great big thank you. One of the very last things she said to me before I unceremoniously decided I really did not want to see her anymore was that there were books written about adult children of alcoholics, and she recommended that I pick one up and read it. She thought it would help me. Of course, I heard this as her telling me that I was some kind of a lunatic so it is no small wonder that I decided to stop seeing her.

I also remembered meeting a woman on a blind date at the Spinnaker Restaurant and just sitting and talking. It was the only time we ever met; there was no repeat performance, and I can neither remember her name nor what she looked like. When we were sharing our travelogs of experience in the field of romance, which is one of the rites of passage when you are meeting someone for the first time under blind-date circumstances, she said something rather peculiar. She mentioned

231

that it was always her luck to get stuck with an "adult child of an alcoholic," and things never worked out with that kind of person because they were just too screwed up and had too many unresolved issues to be really available in a relationship. Well, she wasn't talking about me because we had just met and I was doing a rather splendid job of having my most congenial face on, something I could definitely pull off fairly well over the span of a couple of drinks. But there was something about the term "adult child of an alcoholic" that struck a resonant chord on some primitive level inside. Without even knowing I had done so, I filed it away in the "for future reference" department, which was located somewhere in the deeper recesses of my memory.

So there I was on a sunny Sunday morning, once again sitting alone in my kitchen, trying to decide between two very unattractive options, when all of a sudden I remembered the two references to adult children of alcoholics that had so briefly crossed my path and I wondered if maybe, just maybe, my problem really had to do with alcohol? I knew that I hadn't had a drink for more than six years, so it couldn't be my own alcohol consumption that was the problem. But what about this "adult child of an alcoholic" thing that both women mentioned? I began to feel a long-forgotten glimmer of hope because it really seemed to fit on the inside somehow. Therefore, I decided to temporarily postpone the debate of whether I would kill myself right away or take the slow train by drinking myself to death, and I went in search of anything I could find that had been written about the subject at hand.

It didn't take too long before I was able to locate and secure a copy of the book Adult Children of Alcoholics by Janet G. Woititz. This book hit me with the force of a runaway freight train. As I began reading, I had the distinct feeling that some-

Chapter Four - The Outside Reflects The Inside

body had invaded my psyche and had written down everything they found there. I was stunned by how much I fit into the typical profile of adult children of alcoholics and how much of what I was experiencing was commonplace among this particular population. I began to feel a slight glimmer of hope, a possibility of being able to finally wend my way out of the terribly dark and forbidding woods I had inhabited for such a long time. And I commenced to study every word of every paragraph of every page of this book. I did not just read it; I absorbed it like a comatose person receives life sustaining nutrition through an intravenous drip. Bit by bit, piece by piece, concept by concept, I breathed it in and felt the unmistakable flickers of hope it created flash through me and provide me with the strength to keep going.

A couple of weeks after I purchased the book and began to learn about something that held so much promise for me, I found myself talking to David Dodge during the social hour following another service at The Union Church. For some inexplicable reason our conversation drifted around to the subject of adult children of alcoholics, a subject with which David was quite familiar. He shared with me that both of his parents were alcoholics and that he had a very difficult time dealing with some of the effects growing up in an alcoholic household had on his life as an adult. It just so happened that his wife, Susan, was within earshot of our conversation and came over to tell me that there were meetings for adult children of alcoholics held every Sunday night at the Unitarian Church right down the street. I was floored. I had stumbled, through no fault of my own, onto something that was the next right thing for me, and I had nothing to do with it. God was once again moving me along in the right direction, and all I had to do was lift up my feet and ride the wave.

I soon began to attend the Sunday night meetings of adult children of alcoholics and found out that the meetings were sanctioned by Alanon, the organization that was formed in the wake of Alcoholics Anonymous. Alanon was meant to be a support mechanism for people who were seriously affected by the drinking of a close family member. I learned there were actually quite a few meetings every week in the towns around Stow, and I began to meet and develop relationships with people who had many difficulties similar to my own. But the single most important thing I learned as a result of attending these ACOA (adult children of alcoholics) meetings was that alcoholism is a disease. Once again, it was something I did not know. And I didn't know that I did not know.

I learned that alcoholism is a physical, mental, and spiritual disease that destroys people, ruins families, and causes much pain and destruction. I also learned that it was possible for both the suffering alcoholic and the family members so profoundly impacted by the fallout from this insidious disease to actually recover their lives and live fully by learning and following the principles of the Twelve Steps.

I spent much time over the ensuing weeks thinking about the disease I had known nothing about, even though I had grown up with an alcoholic father. The only thing I knew about Alcoholics Anonymous was that my father would not go. Yet I was only making a little bit of progress; I didn't seem to be making the dramatic shifts in my feelings I expected to make. Although I was feeling more and more hopeful, I wasn't able to get rid of the constant hum of crazy thinking that always seemed to accompany me. Something was still missing and I just couldn't put my hand on it. I was getting closer, of that I was certain, but there was something just beyond my reach, and I needed to find a way to get there.

Chapter Four - The Outside Reflects The Inside

IT'S ABOUT TIME!

On a rather brisk Thursday morning in the middle of January of 1990, I was driving along route 117, heading east toward another day of work and I was, as usual, out of my mind. Only this day seemed to have a more intense charge to it than most regular days. The chatter in my head was deafening, and I was becoming overwhelmed by feelings of total terror because I thought I would never get to the bottom of whatever was so terribly wrong with me, and hadn't I suffered enough already? The gut-wrenching frustration that had become a way of life for me was back again even though I had begun to feel a little bit of relief as a result of attending the ACOA meetings. But now I was starting to feel worse, probably because I expected instantaneous sanity and it was not happening as fast as I would have liked.

Somehow, on this particular morning in January, while driving toward another unfulfilling day in the paper business I had begun to dislike so much, the frustration had reached a heretofore unknown dimension. I felt like a roiling volcano about to erupt in an explosion so intense that Vesuvius would appear to be a mere sneeze. I just couldn't figure out what was wrong with me. I pounded on the dashboard and screamed at the top of my lungs. I pleaded, I begged, looking for the answer that I knew had to be there.

I must have been quite a sight to anyone driving in the opposite direction, but I didn't care. The questions and accusations screamed through my head, and every muscle of my body was tied up in knots so tight it was excruciating. My teeth were clenched to the point that I thought they might shatter and my hands gripped the steering wheel with all the strength I possessed. I screamed and pleaded and pleaded and screamed.

And all of a sudden it was there! The answer was there! It hit me like nothing I had ever felt before. The power of the revelation was totally staggering, yet it felt as gentle as a Spring breeze. "I have a disease," the thought said to me, "I have a disease." And suddenly all of the anger, frustration, pain, fear, and rage were swept aside like they had never existed. I was simultaneously serene and totally excited. I began to laugh and cry at the same time. I had found it, or it had found me. Right out of the crystal clear blue sky, I was given the answer that had eluded me for such a long time. All of a sudden the tribulations of the last six years fell immediately together and made total sense. It was as though the most intricately interlaced rows of dominoes began to fall, one on top of the other, in a magnificently orchestrated and perfectly executed crescendo. One thought - "I have a disease" - coalesced countless years of abject anguish and pain into one quintessentially perfect moment of exquisite relief and release. Thank you, God!

I have a disease. I am an alcoholic. I knew it as intimately and as strongly as I have known anything in my life. I was an alcoholic, and I was entirely delighted to know because now I knew what I could do about it. The following Monday, I attended my very first AA meeting.

I want to stop at this point in the narrative that leads us back to the horrible time I described on route 495 at the beginning of this chapter. Before I get to finally make the point about the outside world being a direct reflection of that which is occurring on the inside, I want to make sure that I illuminate an extremely important underlying theme. This theme underscores virtually every story I tell in this book and is a crucial part of the lesson I am trying to teach. The theme is that of following your nose, listening to the funny little voice inside

Chapter Four - The Outside Reflects The Inside

that will always show you the next right thing to do and letting everything else go.

I did not set out to become a member of Alcoholics Anonymous, although I certainly consumed enough alcohol to qualify for several memberships. It was not the central plan. All I wanted to do was get well. All I wanted to do was permanently put out the fire that was constantly burning in my belly and put an end to the ceaseless stream of poisonous invective that constantly infected my heart, soul, and brain. And it was a stream of "coincidences" I was totally incapable of planning that carried me to the beginning of a life dedicated to healing, truth, and fun. I did not plan it. I did not create it. It was done for me and all I had to do was follow my nose. I have found this to be true in every aspect of my life and, because you and I are not different, you will find that it is true for you as well. All you have to do is be willing to give it a try.

As it turned out for me, finally arriving, alive and physically intact, in the program of Alcoholics Anonymous was really the very beginning of a string of even more amazing coincidences that has brought me to this place and time, writing this book, and communicating with you on a very personal level. I am absolutely certain that, from here, there will be even more "coincidences" that will bring me to more places I am incapable of imagining today. I look forward to the journey.

Everybody can look back at their lives and track the coincidence strings, the events that happen in our lives that have absolutely nothing to do with each other but which, when viewed from a distant enough perspective, clearly form the unmistakable fabric of our lives. These events can be anything from a film that has a particular impact on us, to a person we meet, an athletic event we attend, or a teacher that imparts something we remember many years later when the lesson is immediately useful. Also, I believe that we each have experienced a multitude of coincidence strings that are interrelated and correlated, one with the others, so that we can track any one of them back to the beginning of our lives.

Chapter Four - The Outside Reflects The Inside

AN INCREDIBLE STRING OF "COINCIDENCES"

For the purposes of this particular line of thought and the point I am looking to make, I am going to go back and begin at a point when I was a young alcoholic in training, constantly honing and developing my drinking muscles as though I was training for the Budweiser Hall Of Fame. One fateful evening, the very naive young man I was had intercourse with a very naive young lady. What occurred that evening would be called date rape today, and I would not argue with such a characterization.

The unfortunate result of our evening together was an unwanted pregnancy that neither of us was equipped to deal with. The guilt I suffered from the ensuing abortion was probably the single most compelling factor to push me over the edge into the realm of professional alcoholic. No more amateur stuff for me. Four years later I became engaged to be married and sank deeper into depression, rage, and drinking because at some level I knew it was not the right thing for either of us. Yet, I maintained a rather convincing outside appearance of happiness and contentment. The unrelenting and seemingly progressive nature of the guilt-fueled pain that ruled my life was accompanied by my inability to articulate my suffering to anyone. However, I eventually came to the conclusion that I needed some help and reached for the yellow pages.

This brought me into a relationship with the husband and wife therapists I refer to as the erstwhile therapeutic tag team. I subsequently drank myself through a divorce after only nine months of marriage and actually showed some signs of clearing up. I stopped drinking by way of an agreement with the tag team - and ended up becoming sicker than I ever imagined anyone could be.

Then, living in Dorchester and looking for a shift out of the paper business, I hit upon the idea of a bed and breakfast, which never happened. But it did lead me to looking for a place in the suburbs west of Boston and my encounter with the "Entering Stow" sign. Things moved along a little more quickly from there and I found myself in the white church that I had envisioned, meeting David Dodge, talking with him about adult children of alcoholics in a discussion that his wife, Susan, just happened to overhear. This led to my attending ACOA meetings, finally learning about the disease that so plagued my life, and ending up as a member in good standing of Alcoholics Anonymous. What a ride! And this was the beginning, one of the most benign of my many rides.

Every personal story I share with you contains this underlying theme of amazing strings of coincidences that I could never have predicted, coming together to lead me to places I never could have envisioned but which made more sense for me than I could have imagined. I also know that there is no difference between you and me. So the value to you of reading about my personal foibles, beyond the spiritual lessons I intend to impart and the roadmap to a life of deep and abiding personal peace that I intend to lay down, is that you can use our time together to begin an examination of the strings of coincidences that have brought you to where you are today. Go ahead. You will be truly amazed.

Chapter Four - The Outside Reflects The Inside

MEETING MY SPONSOR

Sunday morning was, without a doubt, my favorite time of the week. It was the day I attended worship service at The Union Church immediately followed by my home-group AA meeting. By the end of this double header I felt protected, loved, and safe. I felt the unmistakable certainty that I was headed in the right direction. Sunday was now a day to sleep a little longer than my usual early-morning rise, and I was no longer spending the entire day creating The Plan. Thank you, God. I no longer felt the need to plan that which was necessary to accomplish all of my crucial-to-the-very-survival-of-the-human-race tasks. Worship service at the Union Church began at 9:00 and ran until around 10:00. This was followed by a social hour, a time to enjoy some excellent coffee, mouth-watering pastries, and get to know the other church members a little bit better. I also decided to take the risk and allow them to get to know me a little bit as well.

Another tradition that has sprung up over the years in AA is to have one member of each group volunteer to be the "greeter" for that particular group. This person generally stands at the entrance of the meeting and welcomes everyone who enters with a handshake and some kind words. It is another way of ensuring that a newcomer has heard at least some words of welcome and encouragement, because most people arriving for the first time are usually too terrified to open their mouths and could possibly end up getting lost in the shuffle.

The man who performed the role of greeter at the Stow Sunday morning meeting was a guy who has never been accused of being tall. He had curly black hair that was trimmed fairly short and had already begun the slow and steady recession from the front of his head toward the back.

HOW TO ENJOY PEACE IN YOUR LIFE EVERY DAY

With his extra long and extra bushy pork-chop sideburns that intersected with his extra long and extra bushy moustache, you never really got around to noticing that he actually had a chin. He was always dressed in some sort of country/western outfit that made him look like an Elvis wannabe. Clearly, he either did not understand or found it hard to accept that he was living in New England, a place that has never had a population of cowboys and wasn't very likely to grow one in the near future. He also had a very gravelly voice that sounded like he might have had something wrong with his voice box or vocal chords, and you really had to strain to hear him when he spoke. But there was an unmistakable spark of life and impishness in his bright blue eyes, and the friendliness, sincerity, playfulness, and peace that lived behind them was clearly visible.

Somewhere in the vicinity of a month after having tumbled into Alcoholics Anonymous, I felt it was about time to take people's advice and begin looking for a sponsor. I needed someone that I could talk to in more depth about what was going on with me, someone to share my entire story with, and someone that had a deeper understanding of the nature of the disease and could give me some more specific advice and insights. I also needed to have a sponsor that had been through the proverbial wringer and come out the better for it, someone that I could not "one up," someone who had gained the insight of having been in worse places than me and had bounced back from the brink of total destruction, presumably having gained much strength and wisdom as a result. I also needed someone who was at least as intelligent and insightful as I was and who had a very good grasp of both inter- and intra-personal dynamics.

But I had a hard time finding someone who lived up to all of

Chapter Four - The Outside Reflects The Inside

my preconditions. Imagine that! Everybody I thought would be a good candidate and with whom I began to have conversations always left me with the feeling that there was something missing. My short list was getting dangerously shorter, and the cream still did not seem to be rising to the top. Nobody stood out from the crowd, at least as measured by my impossible list of necessary qualifications. Oh, did I also mention that the sponsor of my choice should also be very successful in business because I fancied myself the second coming of John D. Rockefeller?

I was getting nowhere fast and I was beginning to despair of ever finding someone I could ask to be my sponsor. It just wasn't happening according to my script and I was not a happy camper about the way this search was developing. Then, one Sunday morning I arrived for the 9:00 church service a little early and instead of sitting in the front row where I usually sat, I plunked myself down somewhere around the middle. This sponsor thing was all I could think of and I needed to get some help with it fast. I couldn't understand why it wasn't coming together so I closed my eyes and blocked my mind to the sounds of people entering the church and taking seats all around me. I concentrated on asking God to help me with my dilemma. I told Him that I knew I needed His help because I certainly wasn't getting anywhere on my own. I also confided in him that I really needed a sponsor because I had reached a point on my own that I could not go beyond and I suspected that with the right kind of help, I was poised to make some dramatic breakthroughs.

And so I sat, concentrating and thinking, thinking and concentrating, until I was brought back to the reality of the moment by the sound of the church organ playing the processional to signal the beginning of the service. When I opened my eyes I was stunned on a multitude of levels by the very first object that clarified in the center of my field of vision. Sitting there in the first row, for the very first time that I knew of because I had never seen him in this church before, was the short Elvis wannabe with the gravelly voice who performed the ritual of greeting people as they arrived at the Sunday morning AA meeting just down the road. I could not believe it; he was all I saw when I opened my eyes and if I had been sitting in my customary first row seat, I would have entirely missed out on this experience.

So I smiled, shook my head at the wonderment of it all, and I said to myself; "looks like I have a sponsor." I also thanked God for taking care of me once again and showing me that everything will turn out ok, no matter what. Sure enough, immediately following the service, without bothering to wait until I got to the AA meeting, and without even bothering to engage him in conversation to establish that he did indeed meet all of my prerequisites, I asked Paul to be my sponsor and was thrilled when he agreed without a second thought.

Paul turned out to be a literal and figurative Godsend. He was the vehicle I used to unload years and years of pent-up emotions, more often than not without having a clue as to where I was going with it or why. He listened with what seemed to be an endless supply of understanding and compassion, as well as a somewhat irreverent sense of humor. Not once did he ever formulate a judgment about me based upon the things I told him. I always felt completely safe in our relationship. The more I spoke to him, the more poison I was able to purge, and the better I began to feel. He was just what I needed.

Chapter Four - The Outside Reflects The Inside

THE END OF THE BEGINNING

Which brings me back to the beginning of this chapter and the instantaneous insanity that went rocketing through my head while I was driving on route 495 that fateful night. This occurred a few months after I began my relationship with Paul and was a direct reaction to his having shared something about his life with me. I can't remember what we were talking about or the reason I felt I needed to talk to him. But I had called him from my car and the conversation somehow got around to the subject of children. Paul told me that when he was an active drunk he had lost two children, one to a rare liver disease and one to SIDS, about which I had not one blessed bit of understanding. My immediate reaction was to accuse him, in my head, of being responsible for the deaths of his two infant children. In my mind, and without verbalizing it to him, I immediately accused him of being a baby killer, and I did not know what to do.

It consumed me and I felt doomed. I knew that I could not possibly keep him as a sponsor because I could never again speak to him without those horrible thoughts somehow coloring everything I said to him and everything he said to me. He had lost all of his credibility with me, and I felt like I had been misled and abandoned. My relationship with Paul was the most important relationship I had ever developed with anyone in my whole life up to that point, and I was in severe danger of blowing it up. I needed help, and this time I asked for it right away.

I called my pastor, David Dodge, the next day and told him I needed to come and speak to him. I told him I was in trouble and I needed his help. So we made an appointment for that afternoon and I went to see him, essentially thinking that I was going to somehow expose Paul, rat him out, so that I could feel a little bit justified in ending our relationship. I was entirely unprepared for what actually happened.

I told David that I thought Paul was a baby killer. Now, David was also a member of Alcoholics Anonymous and had an intimate understanding of how sponsorship worked. He also knew that Paul was my sponsor. Also, he obviously knew Paul because I met Paul in the church of which David was the Pastor. I thought my revelation would knock David's socks off, but Paul's history was something with which David was already familiar. He explained the nature of the diseases that so cruelly took Paul's two children from him at such an early age and explained to me that I couldn't possibly understand the anguish a parent can suffer by the death of one of their children because I never had any of my own. And Paul had lost two. I didn't seem to be getting the support I was looking for, and then he came right out of left field with his next question.

David asked me why it was that I thought Paul was a baby killer. I really didn't understand where he was going with this, but he pressed the issue anyway. Every attempt I made to equivocate, change the subject, or downright refuse to provide an answer, he pressed me. He explained that it was me who was having the poisonous thoughts; they were my thoughts, and they were certainly a rather fierce judgment of another human being. He explained that they were my thoughts and could therefore have nothing to do with Paul; they had something to do only with me. He pointed out a line in the book, *12 Steps And 12 Traditions*, which is published by the Central Service Committee of Alcoholics Anonymous, and related directly to my current situation. This particular passage teaches us that whenever we accuse someone else of something, whenever we so righteously pass judgment on another individual, we are really thinking those thoughts

Chapter Four - The Outside Reflects The Inside

about ourselves. He kept pressing me to look at myself, to put the focus on me rather than on Paul, if I really wanted to get some relief and learn some crucial lessons.

I became indignant. I told him that I couldn't believe he could actually suggest that I thought myself to be a baby killer. I didn't even have any children! But he pressed the issue, and he held on to it like a dog on a bone. He simply would not let it go. I became more and more pissed off and told him that I couldn't believe that I came to him in all sincerity to talk about Paul, which we had done, and now he was only trying to talk about me. I couldn't believe it. What kind of bullshit was this? Thank God he did not let it go, because the truth finally hit me like a ton of bricks. It came out of the deep dark recesses of my mind and rocked me to the core.

I believed that I was a baby killer! And I had been thinking of myself as a baby killer for nearly 15 long and painful years...

...Ever since a naive young man who thought he was some kind of stud got drunk and seduced a rather naive young lady, resulting in a pregnancy that neither of them knew how to handle. Ever since an abortion I arranged for, an abortion I paid for, an abortion that occurred because I lacked the courage to bring the situation to my parents or her parents, or anybody's parents in order to get some help and guidance. Ever since an abortion that occurred because I was emotionally and spiritually incapable of openly and honestly discussing all options. Ever since an abortion that occurred because I was too scared to think straight and I allowed fear to rule my life. Ever since an abortion that occurred because I was totally lacking in character and intestinal fortitude, thus seriously damaging the two of us as a result. Ever since an abortion that occurred because I chose to act without asking for help even though I didn't have the foggiest idea how to go about asking for help because I had never done it before. Ever since an abortion that occurred because we were both extremely naive and ill-equipped to deal with the ramifications of such a major development, even though I fancied myself a rather sophisticated and mature man at the age of 22. Ever since an abortion that occurred because we were both too scared out of our minds to even begin to think about the possibility of doing something different.

Yes, I believed myself to be a baby killer, and I had been carrying that belief around inside for 15 years.

I beat myself with this bat of unmitigated guilt for nearly 15 years and didn't know it. I had discussed the abortion in therapy; I even had the presence of mind to figure out that the abortion was one of my most pressing issues, but the closest I ever came to any kind of understanding of it and my relation to it was to agree to the fact that it wasn't entirely my responsibility. I copped out. I never even put the slightest scratch on the surface of the tremendous fortress of guilt and self-loathing I carried inside myself and with which I very nearly destroyed myself. I actually believed - because I wanted to - that I had left the abortion issue very far behind, until it reared its very ugly countenance on a long and lonely stretch of route 495 some 15 years later. Thank you, God, for my friend and savior, Paul.

Once again, God had placed into my life exactly what I needed to allow me the healing for which I so assiduously searched. Paul was the exact right person, at exactly the right time, with the exactly correct personal history for me to ask to be my sponsor. It was my own guilt I slammed into on route 495, and Paul was unquestionably the touchstone that finally

Chapter Four - The Outside Reflects The Inside

showed me to myself. And the lessons do not stop there; they get better and better, the deeper I look.

Chapter Four - The Outside Reflects The Inside

THE WORLD IS YOUR MIRROR

I learned the world we see outside ourselves is a direct reflection of that which is occurring on the inside. This could be the most important lesson you can take from this book. This lesson and embracing that to which it leads will bring you immeasurably more peace in your personal life than you ever thought possible. This one lesson is the proverbial key to the kingdom because the implications you can draw from it - as well as the opportunities for your practical application of those implications - are virtually endless.

Every single situation that has ever occurred in your life and anything that can possibly happen from now until the moment you draw your last mortal breath, can be more clearly understood by applying this lesson. Further, once you begin to understand that everything you see is merely a reflection of that which exists internally, and once you become willing to embrace all of the ramifications that naturally accrue to this lesson, you will always be able to bring yourself to a place of peace, no matter what is going on in your life.

I couldn't possibly have believed that Paul was a baby killer unless I first believed it of myself, unless I had some evidence (whether or not I was consciously aware that I was using this evidence) of my own guilt. Wait a minute! Does that mean...? Yes, it does. Any time I am involved in accusing anybody of anything, any time I play around with any sort of character assassination in my mind, any time I think less of another individual - no matter what the circumstances might be - it is only because I am projecting my own sense of guilt, self doubt, self loathing, self hatred, and self contempt onto someone else because I mistakenly believe that it will make me feel better. This is of such crucial importance that I need to say it again:

Any time I am involved in accusing anybody of anything, any time I play around with any sort of character assassination in my mind, any time I think less of another individual - no matter what the circumstances might be - it is only because I am projecting my own sense of guilt, self doubt, self loathing, self hatred, and self contempt onto someone else because I mistakenly believe that it will make me feel better.

Any kind of judgement always constricts, makes smaller, and reveals the inner thought structure of the one doing the judging. Therefore, you cannot possibly think less of anyone else without first having thought less of yourself. You cannot possibly attack another individual - whether you do so silently, verbally, or physically - without having first attacked yourself. The good news is that you cannot possibly love another individual without first loving yourself. Our constant goal is to increase the level of self love and decrease the level of guilt.

This is accomplished through forgiveness.

Any time you find yourself judging anyone or anything else, in any way, your very own judgment will point you directly at what you think of yourself. Look for your judgments. Look for your prejudices. Look at what happens to you internally when you think things should be a certain way and they are not. Then place absolutely no value or sense of truth in your judgments except to acknowledge them only for what they reveal about you and how you tend to think about yourself. As soon as you make such an acknowledgment, you have the power to change your thinking and allow the light of truth to melt your self-shrinking judgments away. Freedom must necessarily follow the release of judgments.

Chapter Four - The Outside Reflects The Inside

You can't possibly condemn someone else without having first condemned yourself. There is no escape from or exception to this unassailable truth. Noticing the judgments you make of other people, places, or things every day is a foolproof way of getting to the heart of what you believe to be true about yourself. These judgments can then be brought into the light of your True Self, your inner connection to God, and cast into the oblivion whence they came. Your judgments can set you free as you free yourself of your judgments. Serenity and peace must inevitably follow.

I learned that any time I judge another person, I have first judged myself. This is the good news because all I have to do to get an understanding of how I really feel about myself is to look at how I judge other people. Think about it: Hitler's judgements of the Jewish people had nothing to do with the Jews; it had only to do with Hitler. Assessments made by a white supremacist about people of color have nothing to do with an entire race of people; rather they speak volumes about the person spewing hatred. They perfectly reveal the mountain of guilt and fear that is allowed to live behind that surface of violent and totally restricted thinking. If I am a person who is walking on a path toward greater and greater inner peace and I am thinking that someone else is an asshole, a bigot, or just-plain jerk, then that tells me that I need to be looking at where I believe myself to be an asshole, a bigot, or just-plain jerk.

One of the first lessons in *A Course In Miracles* is that "I give everything I see its value." This is another way of saying that I give everything in my life the meaning it has for me. I place the value on everything I see, from a remarkable piece of art to a rock crab crawling across a beach. For example, 10 people can stand in the Reichsmuseum in Amsterdam and marvel at Rembrandt's The Night Watch and there will most assuredly be 10 entirely unique interpretations given to that one painting. Yet there is only one painting. This is a perfect example of individual people placing different values the same thing. The painting is the painting; it does not change in color or depth, nor does it change in pattern of brush stroke depending upon the viewer. Yet every person who looks at it sees it a little bit differently, because everyone is interpreting the painting according to what is going on inside themselves. This is generally driven by each individual's personal history and particular default settings. Similarly, if I see someone as a loving, compassionate, and genuinely caring individual, it is because I am experiencing my own level of love, care, and compassion. It cannot be any other way.

The world is a mirror, and if you want to get some understanding of where you are and what you are currently thinking, simply take a good look at what this wonderful mirror is reflecting back to you. It has been well said that if you meet three jerks in one day, look in the mirror for the real jerk.

A Course In Miracles teaches us that our enemy is our savior. This is a fairly radical concept. But if you think about it in terms of the outside world being an accurate reflection of that which is happening on the inside, it can then be an entirely freeing concept.

Let's face it: we all know people who, just for the simple fact that they are alive and breathing, bug the living daylights out of us. I have mine, you have yours. They seem to have been put on this earth for the express purpose of fulfilling just this function. We resent them and everything about them, and we seem to enjoy our resentments. Yet, if you ever have the desire to rid yourself of your resentment (because it is your

Chapter Four - The Outside Reflects The Inside

resentment that keeps you prisoner and not the other person) all you have to do is identify exactly what it is about that person you dislike or even hate and then look for those very traits in yourself. Once you find what you are looking for - and I caution you not to stop looking before you find it - simply forgive yourself both for having those things hanging around and for your mistaken judgment of the other person and yourself.

It would be a mistake to berate and deride yourself for being somehow flawed or "less than" once you find what you are looking for. Rather it is just cause for celebration for you have just uncovered an anchor you have been using to drag yourself down without even knowing it.

Chapter Four - The Outside Reflects The Inside

THE ROLE OF FORGIVENESS

Forgiveness is the key that will set you free and keep setting you free. In the fall of 2004, I was sitting in a group of people who gather together every Tuesday night to study *A Course In Miracles*. Somebody was talking about something that he or she was struggling with and all of a sudden the entire abortion saga appeared in my head. However, this time it appeared from an entirely different angle, the proverbial different perspective from which to look at the same issue. It is not so surprising that from the new perspective, the whole scenario looked remarkably different, and I believe I was finally seeing it correctly. It was then that I was able to irrevocably forgive myself, totally and without equivocation. I can honestly tell you the abortion issue and all of its ugly baggage is now gone, as are all minute traces of guilt. I am free. It took real self forgiveness to finally set me free.

If I can do it, so can you.

And the news just keeps getting better. Once you begin to notice more and more (through your own experience and not just because you happened to have read it in a book) that the world you see really is a reflection of that which is happening on the inside, you can then bring yourself to the next level and begin to understand that if this is true for you, then it is true for everyone you know. On a practical level this means that any time anybody is yelling at you, calling you names, insulting you in any way, deriding you, or casting any aspersions on you in any way whatsoever, it has nothing to do with you. Rather, such a situation says volumes about the other person and where they are in their own thinking. They are simply revealing to you the inner torment they are feeling. It is about them, not about you.

Nobody can press your buttons without your permission.

There is no longer a need to take it personally when someone else is attacking you or behaving outrageously toward you. It is not about you. It is simply a manifestation of an internal struggle they are experiencing and for which you just happen to present an available target. If it wasn't you, it would be someone else. Whenever something like this occurs, you can choose to use it as an opportunity to extend compassion, understanding, and forgiveness toward the other person rather than simply defaulting to replying in kind, which only makes you feel worse.

Think about it! If someone else is attacking, insulting, or berating you, it is an opportunity to experience another jolt of personal growth and an increased sense of personal peace! Who would ever think such a thing?

I am not saying that choosing such a response is an easy thing to do. In fact, the first couple of times you do this, you are going to feel like you are dying, which is precisely what is happening. The old you is dying to make room for the new you. When you choose the compassionate response, you are actually expanding and strengthening your Real Self and diminishing the constrictive hold your ego has had over you for your entire life. You have chosen to take a quantum leap toward a more peaceful life, and the ego does not like such a decision. Stay with it and you will be amazed at where you go.

A Course In Miracles teaches that "In your defenselessness, your freedom lies." This means that the day you learn and know there is no need to defend yourself is the day you will be entirely free. The way to get there is by beginning to understand that anytime you attack someone else, it is about you

Chapter Four - The Outside Reflects The Inside

and your own misperceptions, not the other person. This then evolves into an understanding that any time another person attacks you, it is about them and their misperceptions, not about you. Therefore, there is no reason to retaliate.

Taken to the next level, you begin to understand that you are the only one who can attack you. When you eliminate your own attacks upon yourself by recognizing your own mis-perceptions about yourself that engender such attacks and let them go, you begin to understand that you are, and have always been, complete and healed and whole. Which brings us to the next level and the realization that, as an extension of the love of God, you really cannot be attacked at all.

When you reach this level you have come to the peace of God, which is your true essence. It is your core; it is who you really are; it is who you have always have been and who you always will be. And the peace of God cannot be attacked because it does not recognize attack, and that which is not recognized cannot exist. Love recognizes only itself. Peace exists in and of itself and is an integral aspect of the love that created and sustains you, the love of God. This love is all that really exists. All else is illusion, fabricated from the fear-engendering ego, which ceases to exist when love and peace are realized. You must then go to the next level and understand that because you cannot be attacked, there is no need to defend yourself.

"In your defenselessness, your freedom lies."

Which brings us to one of the most important aspects of developing the ability to live a peaceful life: It is learning to have more and more access to the love that is your true essence and living your life from that core. Live from the inside out, rather than from the outside in, so that when the world reflects back to you that which you are offering to the world, all you see is the love that you really are.

CHAPTER FIVE

PEACE IS THE WAY

Chapter Five - Peace Is The Way

"The tendency of man's nature to good is like the tendency of water to flow downwards."

- Mencius
(372 - 289 B. C.)

"No one saves us but ourselves. No one can and no one may. We ourselves must walk the path."

- Buddha

"To laugh often and much; To win the respect of intelligent people and the affection of children; To earn the appreciation of honest critics and endure the betrayal of false friends; To appreciate beauty; To find the best in others; To leave the world a bit better, whether by a healthy child, a garden patch or a redeemed social condition; To know even one life has breathed easier because you have lived. This is to have succeeded."

- Ralph Waldo Emerson

"Independence? That's middle class blasphemy. We are all dependent on one another, every soul of us on earth."

- George Bernard Shaw

Chapter Five - Peace Is The Way

I NEVER SAW IT COMING

The sun was already shining brightly for what promised to be a glorious fall day in the greater Boston area. It was early September and the air had already begun to change. One could detect the unmistakable scent that is the quintessential announcement of the coming of this most colorful season. There is nothing like fall in New England. The sky was amazing - such a bright, clean blue that literally forced you to gaze heavenward as often as you possibly could. It was like looking into the depths of eternity and never quite being able to see as far as it went. I had the unmistakable feeling of humility and awe at the sheer vastness and beauty of it all. I had no idea that my life would dramatically change within the next 15 minutes.

I drove the length of Route 93 south into Boston that morning and, unlike how I usually go about doing things, I actually left the house with enough time to spare. I did not want to be late for this appointment. Route 93 can either be a nightmare of a traffic snarl all the way from southern New Hampshire to downtown Boston, or I can drive the whole way without ever stepping on the brakes. There is no rhyme or reason for this disparity. It is as fickle and changeable as the New England weather. I have experimented with leaving my house at different times of the morning to see if there was a particular window of time that was better than all the rest. The results were completely random, totally inconsequential, and absolutely crazy-making.

This particular morning, with the sky a pure azure blue and the sun shooting laser beams of warmth through the cool clean air, I don't believe the speedometer in my car went below 70 miles per hour. The road was deserted. It was as though the Russian Army had moved in and removed the entire population. I screamed into Boston and I was definitely going to be on time. Everything was going my way.

It was September of 2001, and virtually everything in my life was in a very good place. I had been married to my wife, Elaine, for 8 years and our relationship was, and still is, the most important brick in my foundation. My identical twin daughters, Rebecca and Sabrina, were 6 years old and occupied a very special place in my heart. There is nothing in the world like the love of a daughter for her daddy, and I was fortunate enough to get a double dose of daughterly love. Business was going very well, and my little printing company was making a whole bunch of money. I had been attending meetings of Alcoholics Anonymous and weaving Twelve Step principles into the fabric of my life for nearly 11 years. I had also been studying A Course In Miracles for nearly eight years, so I was in a very good place spiritually as well.

Going to the dentist is generally not considered the height of fun on anyone's enjoyment meter but on this particular morning I was excited about getting there. Now, you are probably going to ask yourself how in the world anyone in their right mind could be excited about going to the dentist, and under normal circumstances I would be right there with you. But these were not normal circumstances, and this was not a normal dentist.

You see, back in the days when the combination of alcohol and youth had me fairly well convinced that I was invincible, I passed out one night while driving my date home from a "beer bust" and I slammed my father's favorite car into a tree. Apparently, the tree did not think I was so indestructible. Trees of solid girth that have been around for a while and

Chapter Five - Peace Is The Way

intend to be around for even longer do not tend to give way much when foreign objects like errant automobiles driven by stupid 19-year-old banana heads crash into them. I can assure you that, 34 years later, said stubborn tree is still standing in the very same place and is none the worse for wear.

I, however, ended up with a double compound fracture of the jaw and many missing teeth. I was truly fortunate not to be killed and was even more fortunate that my date was not killed. By the grace of God, I was given a reprieve that I did not understand until many years later.

So there I was, in early September of 2001, excited to be driving to see Dr, Norman Sheppard, the extremely talented and gifted oral surgeon who was in the process of replacing the very teeth I had lost 28 years before. I had been dreaming of dental implants for quite some time, and I had finally gotten into a financial situation where I could afford to have the work done. Meeting Dr. Sheppard is one of those stories that is replete with coincidences that are not coincidences and quite a bit of humor as well.

The implant work that I went through was very difficult and painful but well worth the bother. The teeth had been gone for so long that the bone in those areas had eroded to the point of being nearly non-existent. In order to successfully place dental implants into anyone's mouth there needs to be a certain amount of bone into which a skilled maxillofacial specialist can drill the supporting posts so that the implant will take and stay in place. Therefore, before anything could be done, the good doctor had to graft some bone into place. Also, because of the deterioration of the bone, my sinuses had fallen and had to be lifted back up and supported, not an easy task for him or for me. But the blessing is that I was in a position to correct some of the damage I had done to myself through the use and abuse of alcohol, and I was very excited about doing just that. Life was good. I felt blessed.

Just a few minutes before 9:00 am, as I was taking the new Leverett Square exit off Route 93, an addition that was a direct result of the "Big Dig" project in the greater Boston area, the sound of a cell phone ringing pierced my reverie. I remember thinking that this had better be important because I was in a very pleasant place in my mind and I was none too pleased to be roused from my rather enjoyable daydream.

My wife was on the phone, and she was telling me something in a very disturbed and excited voice. I recall she was saying something about an airplane that just crashed into the World Trade Center and that it was awful. Now, there is a World Trade Center in Boston and it sits right on a direct flight path to Logan Airport, which is exactly across the harbor from Boston's World Trade Center. Also, Elaine knew that I was on my way to Doctor Sheppard's office in Boston. Therefore, I thought she was telling me the plane crashed into the World Trade Center in Boston and she was warning about the probability of massive traffic jams that would most certainly arise as the city mobilized to deal with a tragedy of such magnitude. Elaine knows I am a native Bostonian and that I know virtually every side street in the city. If anyone knows how to get around traffic in Boston, that person is me.

When I hung up the phone, I was already conducting an all points brain scan to plot a course from my present location to my final destination while avoiding any main roads that would certainly be used for emergency vehicles. In no more than a minute or two, I had the most effective route for me

Chapter Five - Peace Is The Way

to take locked and loaded into the automatic pilot of my driving brain, and I was just about to begin tackling the return route problem when the phone rang again. It was Elaine, and this time she was even more upset than the last time. She told me that a second plane had just been flown into the World Trade Center, and she was going on and on in a somewhat hysterical way. I still did not get it, and I was at least a little perplexed about the fact that I was already in Boston but I hadn't heard even one emergency-vehicle siren.

Finally, she calmed down enough and I became sufficiently ready to listen so that she was able to explain to me that it was not the World Trade Center in Boston that was attacked, but that it was the two buildings of the World Trade Center in New York City. She then went on to explain that it was not an accident, that the two airliners were deliberately flown into the World Trade Center and that it was almost certainly a terrorist attack.

I became immediately enraged. My first words to Elaine after I was able to finally understand exactly what had just occurred were, "Looks like we're at war with someone." Every thought that was flooding my now-overtaxed brain had to do with vengeance, retaliation, and war. I told Elaine that I wanted to hang up and listen to the radio, which is what I did as I drove on in somewhat of a fog toward my appointment with Doctor Sheppard. At least I was still going to be on time.

What happened next has irrevocably changed my life.

Chapter Five - Peace Is The Way

THIS IS MUCH BIGGER THAN ME

As I drove along, not having to shift my pre-planned route of travel at all, I became less and less outraged and more and more calm. Then I noticed a very curious thing. I noticed that the calm was always there, and it had never even wavered. It existed prior to Elaine's initial phone call and it was still there, totally unchanged. I was only just becoming aware of its presence because of the tremendous contrast between it and the noise that was running through my head. It felt as though my mental turbulence was desperately trying to penetrate the sea of peace that existed inside and was not having a very easy time of it. The feeling of peace, the sense of pervading rightness that comes from knowing that everything is how it is supposed to be, had not changed from the very beginning of the first conversation I had with my now distraught wife.

I did not understand what was happening to me. I expected myself to be entirely and totally consumed with unyielding rage and a driving need to strike back immediately. Such thoughts were running through my head at an impressive rate but I could not find a similar sentiment in my heart or my soul. It simply was not there; it did not exist, and it was a very odd experience. It was as though my initial outrage was sitting on top of my now finely honed instinct for peace like a thin veneer, attached to, but not part of, the solid block of wood underneath.

As I continued driving toward my destination and I watched this mini drama unfold, I understood that I was actually seeking congruence, a total agreement between my heart and my head, a condition that I had come to believe in. If I had congruence then I knew, no matter what the situation, I was headed in the right direction. I thought the congruence I was seeking would manifest itself by having the thirst for revenge overcome everything else and leave me in a pleasant state of totally violent intention. In fact, I was trying to push myself in that very direction.

I wanted to be mad. I wanted to want to kill. I wanted to feel like striking back in ways that would be even more memorable than that which had just occurred. But the more I looked, the more I understood that my internal feeling of peace was not going to yield to the mania in my head. I was even more surprised when I finally realized that just the opposite was taking place. The initial jolt of outrage and consuming desire for retaliation was rapidly receding in the face of something significantly more powerful and abundantly more real.

Yes, just the opposite was happening, and there wasn't anyone more surprised on the face of the planet than I was as I drove along looking as though I had seen a ghost. The congruence I was looking for was beginning to emerge; the alignment between that which lived in my heart and soul and the thoughts that ran through my head were indeed beginning to line up, one with the other. But not in the way I thought it would happen. The incessant noise about bombs, death, and destruction that had occupied the gray matter of my brain rapidly receded in the face of the remarkably cleansing thoughts of love and peace emerging from the core of who I am.

And it wasn't as though the violent thoughts I had been entertaining actually receded. They simply disappeared without a trace, like they had never actually existed in the first place. They just dissipated without a sound and without a fight, like a morning fog hugging the cool ground vanishes when the life-giving rays of the warm sun penetrate the unsuspecting mist. And all of this took place in a matter of mere seconds.

Chapter Five - Peace Is The Way

Darkness cannot live in light. Hatred cannot exist where peace abides.

The instinct for peace that I had been building in myself ever since the day I made the irrevocable decision that I would have peace in my life no matter what, had taken on a life of its own. It was providing the congruence I sought in a very different way than the one I tried to bring about. And there didn't seem to be anything I could do about it, save to sit back and watch the show.

I was astounded, amazed, and thunderstruck. I drove along with my jaw literally on my chest. My eyes were wide open in utter amazement as the flood of peace and tranquility washed over me. All the while, sitting very subtly in the background but not outside the scope of my awareness was the complete understanding that my entire life had just changed, that everything would be different from this day forward, that up was down and down was up, and that pigs really could fly.

(The next time I had such a feeling, although nowhere near as intensely as I did on the morning of 9/11/2001, was the day in October of 2004 when the Boston Red Sox finally won the World Series.)

I became totally consumed with an abiding sense of wonder and awe. It was the most exhilarating feeling I had ever experienced, and I was abundantly clear that this feeling did not emanate from me. Its source was a power much greater than myself, and I couldn't help but feel an unmistakable connection and oneness with that power. At the same time I was uniquely aware that I was definitely in the process of achieving my lifelong goal of coming closer to the person that God originally intended for me to be. And the only choice I really had was to embrace it. So I continued to keep driving toward my ultimate destination, watching in absolute astonishment as this most unusual drama played itself out inside me. The more I watched, the more I understood that my instinct for peace and forgiveness had really become the unshakable foundation supporting the structure of my life, and I was well beyond grateful. I was awestruck.

I had actually arrived at a place where I knew with every fiber of my being that peace was really the only solution to everything. Like a fire that lacks the fuel to keep it burning, my initial need for retaliation simply fizzled away because there wasn't anything inside me to support those negative sentiments. They just didn't have any legs. At the same time, the strength and power of my instinct for peace and forgiveness grew from the center of my being and ever so gently melted all adverse thoughts and emotions until I was filled with nothing but light and love. And I knew that my life would be different from that day forward.

The experience reminds me of the Steven Spielberg movie, Close Encounters of the Third Kind. When the people who had been having such clear and vivid internal images finally saw the terrain they had been imagining in person, they began to feel a certain sense of relief and fulfillment. When the alien spaceship descended from the sky, they knew they had arrived at the place they were supposed to be, the place they had been drawn to by a power greater than themselves, the place where they belonged. They and everyone else who witnessed the actual alien craft land and open its doors knew right down to their toes that the world would henceforth be a very different place for them.

As I sit here typing away on my laptop computer three-and-a-half years later, I can still feel the gratitude and awe with which I was filled that day. And it is as amazing now as it was then.

Chapter Five - Peace Is The Way

THE POSITION OF PEACE IS THE POSITION OF STRENGTH

Today I enjoy the cleaner perspective that both time and distance afford, and I have a better understanding of the experience I had on September 11, 2001. Today I know that what happened to me was merely a microcosmic example of what can happen on a global scale. I am not special, and I am not unique. I was not singled out by God to bring a message of peace to mankind. I had simply chosen to make myself ready to connect to that which has always lived inside me and that which lives inside every person on the planet as well. It is not within the scope of my mere human ability to imagine what the world would look like if everyone on the planet felt the same way. But I do know that it is not only possible - it is inevitable.

We were all created by God to reflect the light and love that is His essence. It is our reality and our only reality. All else is illusion. And there isn't anything anybody can do to change this timeless truth. The love and peace of God has always been there and will always be there, patiently waiting for you to come home. By its very nature it cannot force itself upon you, and it cannot make you believe that it is there. You can merely decide one day, just as I decided, that there must be another way. As soon as you make a commitment to seek the alternative that most assuredly will bring you to the love and peace from which you came. You will discover that it is all you will allow in your life, come what may.

I had decided many years before the events of 9/11 that I was going to have peace in my life, and ever since I made that decision I had been working on eliminating the blocks to peace that I tend to create. One at a time. I realize now, three-and-a-half years later, that it took every single decision I made to seek the answer that would bring the most peace to put myself in a position where I would be ready to receive the gifts that came my way on 9/11.

As I drove toward my appointment with Doctor Sheppard, the trauma initially inspired by the events of 9/11 completely disintegrated in the face of the consummate power of the Love of God. I finally knew that there would eventually be peace on earth because it is all that really exists. I became acutely aware that the position of peace is the single most powerful position and that all the bombs, weapons, and anger that can be made by the hand of man fade to nothing when exposed to the light that is the love and peace of God.

Love and peace have been freely given to us by God. They are not made by the hand of man. Having not created love and peace, we are totally unable to change, alter, manipulate, or destroy them. However, we can choose to allow them to enter our consciousness and be the beacons that light our way through the seemingly troubled world that man created. Neither Joseph Stalin, Adolf Hitler, Saddam Hussein, nor George W. Bush can remotely touch or in any way alter the existence, pervasiveness, or inevitability of the Love of God. It is simply not possible. It cannot be done. Because it is of God and not of man. It is therefore eternal and not subject to the machinations of the human race, the stuff that everyone thinks is so important. The Hitlers of the world will come and they will go. But nobody has the power to remotely alter the Love of God that created and sustains us. Love can neither be created nor destroyed. It can't be manipulated, changed, or altered in any way. Love can only be remembered, accepted, and embraced. The peace of God is sitting there waiting for everyone in the world to come home, just like I finally came home on 9/11/2001.

Chapter Five - Peace Is The Way

Please understand that the peaceful response is not one of impotence, abdication, or acquiescence. It is not the chickenshit response of accepting the unacceptable nor is it a position lacking in courage or fortitude. In fact, just the opposite is true. The position of peace is the most powerful and courageous one to take. It is also very often the most unpopular and ridiculed because people do not yet understand that the answer to all their dreams and desires are encompassed therein.

"Father, forgive them for they know not what they do" is one of the most profoundly loving and ultimately peaceful statements ever made. It was the embodiment of Christ's innate understanding that there wasn't anything anyone could do that could remotely touch him. He was beyond the hand of man, and he knew it because he lived and breathed the acceptance of love and peace as the only true way to exist. He did not say these words because he thought it was such an outrageous crime to kill the son of God. Think about it. How can you possibly kill the idea of God? Such a notion is palpably preposterous. He knew that the Roman soldiers and all the rest of his tormentors were as much the sons and daughters of God as he was. The only difference was that Christ knew it, and they did not.

He knew beyond a shadow of a doubt that if the people who were clamoring for his crucifixion understood they were the sons and daughters of God, they would not feel compelled to end Christ's life. Jesus would not have presented such a threat to their ingrained thought system and lust for personal power. They believed that by putting him to death, his message of unconditional love would die with him. They were wrong.

Christ uttered those immortal words (and they were indeed

immortal because they came from a place that transcends everything) while he was hanging on the cross and was very close to taking his last mortal breath. He understood that the people before him believed that by killing him they would silence the voice for truth, love, and peace. They couldn't live with the incongruity between someone teaching them to love their neighbor as themselves and the way they had been trained to think all their lives. It must have seemed so much easier for them to simply remove the one aspect of this incongruity they believed they had the power to remove.

By crucifying Jesus Christ, they chose the easier, softer way. To do otherwise would have required that they examine themselves and their motivations and beliefs. It would have been necessary to take a serious look at the fear that permeated their every waking moment and having found it, they would then have to do something about removing it. They thought that by killing a man, you can kill an idea, like removing the source of a foul odor removes the odor. They were wrong. They believed in the power of the sword to vanquish anyone or anything that didn't necessarily agree with them, something that man has been doing since the dawn of time.

Christ's words were an accurate reflection of his understanding that people who believe it is possible to destroy both the reality and the idea of love simply by taking the breath away from one man are only condemning themselves to lives of additional and unnecessary pain. He also knew that nobody can silence the voice for peace and love because it is as much the essence of the persecutors as the persecuted. The only difference is that one knows it and the other doesn't. Therefore, Christ's words were more of a lament for the poor people who were, unbeknownst to themselves, depriving themselves of the unmitigated joy that living life from a place of love and peace can bring.

Chapter Five - Peace Is The Way

On the day of his crucifixion, Christ was clearly ensconced in the position of peace. His statement had nothing to do with any perceived harm that might be caused to his physical body because he knew he was not his body. His statement had nothing to do with the fact that he was about to draw his last breath because he knew that death does not exist. And his statement had nothing to do with fear because he understood the end of one's physical body did not mean the end of life.

When Christ forgave everybody for not knowing what they were doing, he released them and he released himself at the same time.

And so we come to the time of the proverbial gut check. As a result of the previous discussion, there are a number of very interesting questions now on the table. They are:

Is the position that Christ took on the cross, the peaceful position, one of weakness or of strength?

Is the position that Christ took on the cross, the peaceful position, one of cowardice or of courage?

Is the position that Christ took on the cross, the position of love, one of abdication or power?

If you answered strength, courage, and power to the previous questions, then you are absolutely correct. You are also totally screwed because if you truly believe those answers, then you must measure everything you do for the rest of your life against a very different frame of reference than the one you probably carried into page one of this book. You have no choice because once you awaken the peace giant inside, there isn't anything you can do over the long term to quiet it down.

The only choice you have left is to feed, clothe, and nurture him so that he will continue to grow unabated. Herein lies your complete and total freedom.

People like Gandhi, King, and Mother Teresa learned the value of non-violence, the power of the peaceful position, and the timelessness of the idea of love. It is how they have been able to so positively influence so many millions of people. It is also why the legacies of people like Hitler and Stalin will fade into the insubstantial mist from which they were initially created.

THE JUSTIFICATION FOR WAR

It took the events of 9/11 to bring to my conscious mind a more complete grasp of the value and impregnability of the peaceful response. It took what the vast majority of people in the world consider to be a horrific tragedy for me to finally understand that peace is inevitable because peace and love are all that is real. And it took the events of 9/11 to show me in ways so abundantly clear that responding to violence with violence simply perpetuates the cycle of violence which has never - and will never - solve anything. The only response that can possibly bring about real and permanent change is the peaceful response, and it is the single most powerful position available. However, it is not the easiest decision to make. It is also a decision that is consummately and popularly mis-understood.

Choosing to live a life of peace is not unlike an athlete deciding she wants to compete in the Olympics and win a gold medal. The first thing she needs to do is make a decision to go for the gold. Then she needs to make a commitment to the rigors of doing whatever is necessary to attain the goal. She gets up every morning at 4:30 am when the rest of humanity is fast asleep and couldn't be bothered living such a disciplined life. As soon as she hears the alarm bell ring, she knows she has a choice. She has come to understand that the difference between success and failure lies in the decision she makes every day to plant her feet on the floor as soon as that alarm clock sounds, no matter what. Even if she is dog tired and is losing the struggle to force her eyes open, those feet need to go to the floor because she has made a promise to herself.

The thought of turning over and going back to sleep is very often mighty inviting. Who would ever know if she skipped just one day? But she also understands that winning the race does not occur after the starting gun goes off. Rather, the race is won every day she trains herself, so that it is over long before it begins. On the day of the race, she is virtually going through the motions. It is the training she does today and the discipline she brings to her life today that will get her through the race tomorrow. It is the training and the individual decisions to support the training she makes today that puts her in a position to allow the race to take care of itself.

After she wins the gold medal, there is nobody more surprised than she is when she discovers it was never really about the medal. It is only then she learns that what she has actually been working on has been building something she can use for the rest of her life, in everything she does. She is singularly struck to figure out that going through the process rather than winning the race is the highest value. And she is amazed to finally conclude that what she had previously thought of as an end was really only the beginning.

Prior to September 11, 2001, I had been studying *A Course In Miracles* for many years and had been immersed in the Twelve Steps of recovery for even longer. Having begun walking down the path of seeking the truth, I eventually arrived at a place of critical mass where I decided that I would accept nothing less than peace in my life. I subsequently made a commitment to that decision. From that day forward I had been exercising and training my peace muscles, so that when 9/11 arrived I was ready to receive an entirely different message than I would otherwise have received.

Ever since the day I decided that I was going to have peace in my life, no matter what, I began to build an unshakable foundation. Every single small decision I made since then to follow

Chapter Five - Peace Is The Way

the path of peace by making irrevocable situational choices to seek the most peaceful solution, had created, unbeknownst to me, an internal mechanism that now refused to accept anything but peace. On the morning of 9/11 I arrived at what should have been a major fork in the road of my life only to find that the fork did not exist. There was only one path that lay ahead, and I knew with every fiber of my being that this was the path of peace.

All of a sudden I understood that answering violence with violence has never produced positive results. Such a response has only served to create the seeming excuse for the next retaliation, and so on. It finally dawned on me that every single war that has ever been fought since the dawn of man has only succeeded in sowing the seeds for the next inevitable conflict. Check it out. Look at history, and you will see that what I am saying is an unassailable truth, as all truth is unassailable. It doesn't matter the perspective from which you seek to justify any war. The justification used will always contain the justification for the next war as well.

Remember, the justifications for war on an international level are but variations on the theme of justifications for interpersonal conflict. Pre-emptive international strikes are the same as pre-emptive interpersonal strikes. Arguments never produce winners, but they are great at producing resentments, which sow the seeds of the next inevitable conflict. Real forgiveness is the only cure.

As an example, let's take a slightly closer look at one of the justifications used for fighting World War II. I hear many people say that the Second World War was a just war because it removed Adolf Hitler and put an end to the Holocaust. Unfortunately, this argument ignores the historically proven fact that it was the First World War, more popularly known at the time as "The War to End All Wars," as well as the "peace" treaty that formally ended said "justifiable" war, which gave rise to the possibility of Adolf Hitler in the first place. All he did was walk into the breach that was provided by the conditions left over from the end of the First World War. Without the First World War, Adolf Hitler's rise to power would not have been possible.

Also, let us not forget that it was World War II, the so-called justifiable war, that provided the fertilized soil from which grew the Soviet Union and the murderous reign of Joseph Stalin. You will remember that England and France declared war on Germany after the invasion of Poland. Yet, at the end of the war, Poland was occupied by the Soviet Union. One conqueror traded for another conqueror. Also, bear in mind that the Holocaust and the treatment of the Jews at the hands of the Nazis weren't considerations as part of the "justification" of World War II, either before or during the war. It was also the unique dynamic created by the Second World War that provided Mao the opportunity to sweep across mainland China and subjugate its people. Untold millions died at the hands of the Chinese Communists.

Interestingly enough, the spark that eventually ignited the flame of World War I was struck in the Balkans. The end of World War I saw the break up of the Balkan states into many different entities. I will point out that the Balkans was the scene of another terrible conflict in the early 1990s, and this conflict was a direct result of issues that were never settled by the conflagration of World War I. They were in fact exacerbated by the treaty and land distribution policies that formally ended the war. Yet the fear that fans the flames of ethnic intolerance and hatred is still rampant in the region, like an acci-

Chapter Five - Peace Is The Way

dent looking for a place to happen. As I understand it, the Balkan conflict is today threatening to erupt yet again. And the justification for war is what again?

Unbeknownst to most Americans is the fact that the American involvement in Vietnam, as well as the Soviet invasion of Afghanistan, were direct results of different seeds that were sown during the Second World War and before. It does not take a genius to draw the lines from Afghanistan through the Middle East to 9/11, back to Afghanistan, and eventually to the American invasion of Iraq. Also interesting is the fact that Iraq was not even a country and did not become a nation until the treaty that ended World War I. It was a direct result of the conquering nations deciding to carve up the Middle East for their own political and economic purposes. Also lost in the confusion is the small detail that it was American money that funded and equipped Saddam Hussein in the Iraq/Iran war. The Iraqi military buildup that brought about the invasion of Kuwait and the first Gulf War was paid for by the American people.

The only question that remains is where the next conflict will be. If you listen very closely, you can already hear the rhetorical build up of a case against Iran. It is quite conceivable that some very believable "justifications" will be directed toward a mostly naive American public before the next inevitable war begins.

Remember, nothing changes if nothing changes. Insanity is doing the same things over and over again but expecting different results.

If one were to take the simple perspective of looking at the events of 9/11 purely in the context of loss of human life, then you have to accept that such a cost pales in comparison to many other episodes of man's willingness to destroy man. The events of 9/11 are nothing compared to the firebombing of Dresden in World War II, the racial genocide in Rwanda that the world hasn't been able to muster even a whisp of outrage about, the Holocaust that was perpetrated by Adolf Hitler and the German war machine as the world turned its collective head, the wholesale slaughter of millions of innocent civilians by Joseph Stalin, or the annihilation of the Native American population by the inexorable expansion of white "civilization." Placed in historical context, the events of 9/11 are but blips on the screen.

But the context is wrong. To compare one negative thing to another and then use a favorable comparison to cast it in the light of acceptability is just another way of perpetuating the lie. Remember, the same fear that causes someone to plan and carry out such acts as the events of 9/11 is the same fear that drives a man to beat his wife. It is the same fear that moves a parent to beat a child. It is the same fear that causes entire populations to scream for retaliation and revenge when it perceives it has been outrageously attacked. And it is the same fear that is the stock in trade of the ego, which is the small self that is no part of the Self at all. But it is the ego that we more often than not place in the position of most honored and respected guest at the dinner table.

The retaliation response is so well inculcated into our collective psyche that is has become the only acceptable and expected option. It lives in the "A" drawer, and there just doesn't seem to be any other drawers available from which to extract a viable alternative. Unless, of course, one is willing to look beyond the borders of the familiar. It is the idea of war as the only logical alternative that needs to be erased in the

Chapter Five - Peace Is The Way

minds of man in order to eliminate the actuality of war and all the attendant suffering.

If you take a dispassionate step back from all of the rhetoric that surrounds 9/11 and look at what has transpired since then, you can't help but notice that history is indeed repeating itself. The prime perpetrator of the 9/11 attacks has yet to be brought to justice. The American military is bogged down in a quagmire that is as much political in nature as it is military. The quagmire has no end in sight and will cost many more lives and billions of dollars. The justifications for the action that have come out of the American administration are incredibly reminiscent of the Vietnam War. People who raise their voice against the war in Iraq are branded as unpatriotic on the low end and lovers of terror on the high side. This is a little like being called a pinko commie fag during the Vietnam War. It is the same old, same old. And it really is becoming a little bit boring.

Yet I am the first person to tell you that everything happens for a reason and the reason is always flowing toward the good for everyone involved. Neither one person nor a nation of people can stop the flow of the propensity of mankind to move slowly but inexorably in the direction of the greater good. That which is happening today in the Middle East is happening for a reason. I cannot tell you what it is because I have only a very limited perspective from which to observe, and the batteries in my crystal ball ran dry many years ago. But I do know, and I know this with every fiber of my being, that everything always works out right in the long run. It always has and always will. What we are currently experiencing is a mere blip on the screen of humanity. This fact is much greater than any individual, political party, or nation. And it is a fact in which I have unyielding faith.

The idea of war will begin a long and slow demise on the day enough people stand up and simply refuse to go there any more. I do not know when that will occur, but occur it will. As I said in Chapter One;

Peace is inevitable.

Pain and suffering are optional.

The choice is yours.

On an individual basis we get to choose how we are going to live our lives every day. The quality of our lives is determined by the decisions we make. The idea of war as an acceptable alternative can only be eliminated one person at a time, one day at a time, one thought at a time. War, as an accepted international institution, will only go away when enough people decide to eliminate war as an acceptable personal institution. The idea of war will disappear when enough people decide they are going to accept nothing but peace in their personal lives. It is my sincere hope that I will be around long enough to see it happen.

But until such time as the idea of peace as the only acceptable alternative becomes our collective reality, please allow me to engage in some very wishful thinking.

Chapter Five - Peace Is The Way

WHAT IF

But what if....

The United States of America found itself in a very unique position on 9/10/2001. The Cold War was over and America had emerged as the last remaining superpower left on earth. America wielded historically unprecedented worldwide economic influence. The American military was the most awesome and capable fighting machine the world had ever known and possessed the potential to project power anywhere and at the time of its own choosing.

Therefore, on 9/12/2001 the American people and political leadership were in a very unique position, historically speaking, to influence world affairs in a very different way than any country ever had the ability to do. We were in a position to do something the world has never, ever seen and which would have brought about immediate and profound worldwide change.

I ask you to imagine the following scenario. I understand the easy thing to do is immediately think of ways this little fantasy of mine could never happen. Anybody can think of reasons something can't be done. Doing so is not a challenge and is a manifestation of the default type of thinking that lives on the surface of the conscious mind and is largely dictated by the ego. I am asking you to go beyond your initial doubts and outright rejections to ask yourself, why not? I am asking you to allow my little bit of wishful thinking to penetrate the initial knee-jerk negative response that lives on the surface. Allow your Real Self to consider the possibilities. If there were enough "why nots" in the world, then perhaps what I am about to put forth wouldn't necessarily be a fantasy.

Imagine the American president walks to a bank of microphones to make his first public speech in the wake of the attacks of 9/11. The name of the president is not important because this is, after all, a fantasy. The man in the position could be George W. Bush, Bill Clinton, George Washington, or Alfred E. Newman. Neither the name nor the personality matters. What does matter is what he says.

The speech is televised live all around the world on a bazillion different radio and television stations and is simultaneously translated into hundreds of languages. The world holds its collective breath as he walks to the microphone in anticipation of what he is going to say, what the repercussions are going to be, and who is going to be paying the ultimate price for having launched such a horrific attack on the American mainland. Everyone seems to know what is coming and the only thing in question, really, is the level and ferocity of the American response.

The president calmly walks to the microphones, and the first thing the newscasters, pundits, and prognosticators notice is how relaxed he appears to be. Everyone comments on the fact that the president actually looks rested and upbeat. Commentators are whispering into their microphones just like the sportscasters covering the Masters Golf Tournament. Everyone fully expected he would look like something the cat dragged in and forgot to drag back out again. The president surprised everyone because he was supposed to look extremely bedraggled, like a man who stayed up all night with the weight of the world sitting squarely on his shoulders and inexorably crushing him, bit by precious bit. Instead, he looks positively buoyant, and this is only the first surprise.

Chapter Five - Peace Is The Way

He begins by acknowledging the members of Congress who were present, the American people he was elected to represent on the world stage, and viewers from around the world. Then he speaks.

"Yesterday the entire world community was shocked by the sudden, violent, and premeditated assault on the World Trade Center in New York City. While the attack was directed primarily at America and the American people, it was really an attack against everyone seeking to live in freedom and safety all around the world. This kind of behavior on the part of certain individuals seeking to export their own ideas of how the world ought to be run will not be tolerated by the American people, nor will it be tolerated by freedom-seeking people the world over.

Our intelligence sources have positively identified Osama Bin Laden and the Al Quaeda terrorist network as the perpetrators of this monstrous attack, and I am here to tell you that such tactics directed against the people of The United States of America cannot and will not succeed.

Now, I know you are all thinking that I am talking about America's awesome military might as the reason attacking America in such a fashion is doomed to failure. In many ways this is true, and I am not going to deny the fact that we have the ability to respond in kind on a scale that would make the attacks of 9/11 pale in comparison. But that is not what I am alluding to.

For 200 plus years the United States of America has been a living, breathing experiment in constitutional democracy. The Founding Fathers found it in their eternal collective wisdom to invest the real power in this country firmly in the hands of the people, ordinary people like the brave firefighters who gave their lives yesterday while trying to rescue others from certain disaster. The real power in this country lives in the hearts of the American people who have the ability, and exercise the ability, to disagree with their elected officials. If the disagreement is widespread enough, they further have the ability as well as the responsibility and the right to replace them in the next election.

The real power in this country is not the military power we clearly possess; rather, it is the collective power of a people who crave the freedoms that have been guaranteed to them by the U. S. Constitution. The Constitution is much greater than any political party or special interest group, and it invests ultimate power in the hands of the people.

If Osama Bin Laden or any other power-hungry terrorist who comes along thinks he can conquer America and the American people by blowing up a couple of buildings and threatening to blow up some more, he is sadly mistaken. They clearly do not get it. They do not understand, and I am certain they are not capable of understanding. Well, I am here to tell anyone who might think they can hurt America by bombing buildings, killing innocent people, or launching terrorist attacks of any kind against us, that you really cannot hurt us on a scale that you think is possible. It is an impossibility that only a nitwit could ever believe.

There isn't a power on earth that can conquer America because America is, first and foremost, an idea. It is an idea that millions of people from around the world have flocked to our shores to participate in. It is an idea that transcends politics and religious beliefs, and it is an idea that cannot ever be conquered or subjugated by anyone.

Chapter Five - Peace Is The Way

Think about it: Bin Laden lives in a cave halfway around the world. Do you think that a small-thinking cave-dweller is an actual threat to the internal security of the United States of America? I find such a notion to be absolutely ludicrous. Does anybody seriously believe that Bin Laden or any other individual has the power to destroy the greatest system of democracy the world has ever known just by destroying a couple of buildings and killing innocent people? I sincerely doubt it. I will not give one shred of credibility to Bin Laden or any other terrorist who thinks they can bring down that which is so much greater than the sum of all the individuals living in this country.

I have given much thought to the course of action America should take, and I have come up with a rather different idea than most people viewing this broadcast could have predicted. The way I see it, America today is in a historically unique position. We are militarily the most powerful nation on earth. On the economic front we are one of the most prosperous nations in the world, and we wield significant international political influence. I have always believed that with power comes responsibility.

America is in a very strong position in the world, and we have the ability to lead the world in a very different way than any nation has ever led the world before. We are strong enough internally and we are strong enough externally. We have been thrust into a situation not of our creation, and we have an opportunity as a result to significantly change the way the world does business.

As I thought about the appropriate response for the American people to take, I considered the fact that violence only begets more violence. And I cannot think of one situation where violence ever solved anything. Do you think that Bin Laden's attack on the World Trade Center got him any closer to conquering America? Do you think that Bin Laden's attack on the World Trade Center has gotten him any closer to changing the way America operates in the world? Of course not. Violence will never solve anything.

Therefore, I will not answer this senseless and futile act of violence with even more violence. As far as I am concerned, the idea of war and all its ugly ramifications stops right here, right now. I will not go there, and I will not lead the American people down a path I believe will only lead to more of the same. International violence must stop, and the idea of terrorism and war as legitimate answers to anything must stop right here, right now.

I believe we must begin a dialog in earnest with the people of different cultures around the world, and I firmly believe we must engage in a long-term, fruitful exchange with the people of the Islamic world. These dialogs must proceed right away and must have the attainment and sustainment of world peace as the only objective. I can't believe anybody who really thinks about it will agree with Bin Laden that bombing buildings for the sake of killing innocent people is a good thing to do. In reality it leads nowhere. Peace, on the other hand, can lead everywhere.

If Bin Laden is any kind of a man and he has a legitimate gripe with the United States of America, he can talk about it at his trial. He is wanted for murder and he will be hunted and brought to trial. Make no mistake about it: It does not take courage for a man to sit in the relative safety of his cave and send others to murder innocent people. What it takes is a common coward, a run-of-the-mill criminal. Bin Laden is no hero. He has set himself up as the leader of the people of

Chapter Five - Peace Is The Way

Islam, but he is nothing but a small-minded murderer and can do no lasting good for anyone. Only Bin Laden's ego benefits from his actions.

I propose the world live in peace from this day forward and I am willing to meet with anybody at any time to further the cause of world peace. Please do not think that this proposal comes from a position of fear or weakness. It most assuredly does not. Quite the contrary. I am proposing such a radical measure precisely because the United States of America is in a position from a standpoint of internal strength and international influence to make and actually carry out such a radical and world-changing proposal.

International peace is the greatest economic motivator imaginable, and there is no limit to what we can accomplish with the world community working together toward the common goal of peace and prosperity. But in order for such a thing to occur, someone must lead the way. We are in a unique position to do so, and it is my strong belief that we should go there right now, without delay.

In order for terrorists to succeed, they must frighten people. Neither Bin Laden nor any other terrorist can frighten us because what we have is so much greater than anything he can do to us. Bin Laden does not frighten me nor does he frighten America because we know he is nothing but a playground bully, and his playground has just gotten much smaller. He is a non issue.

From this day froward, the United States of America pledges itself and commits itself to waging international peace, come what may. The time has come for us to move together toward this noble and eminently reachable goal.

Thank you, and God bless you all."

You must admit, it is a fairly interesting little fantasy. But it also creates some rather compelling questions. What do you suppose the world would look like today if the American president really did make a speech like the one I put forth on these pages? I do not know the answer to the question, but I do know it would look very different than the one we see today. It sure would have been interesting as well as exciting to see what could have happened.

I have mentioned many times in this book that the macrocosm and the microcosm are the same. One nation standing up on the international level and declaring it will wage nothing but peace is the same dynamic as an individual standing up and deciding he or she will allow nothing but peace in their personal lives. Inasmuch as the individual's life would dramatically change for the better just as mine has done, I must then believe the life of the intrepid nation would dramatically change for the better as well.

Anyone can come up with a million different reasons as to exactly why such a peace-oriented response would never work and those reasons would sound quite convincing. I am also certain that underlying all of the reasons to pursue the time honored tradition of a tooth-for-a-tooth is a prevailing current of fear. All of those reasons would merely be variations on the same theme that has always held war as justifiable. It is just too terrifying to think about doing something so radically different. What if it didn't work? Well, what we have been doing for the last few hundred years hasn't worked very well, so what do we actually have to lose?

It is much easier to default to that which we know, that which

Chapter Five - Peace Is The Way

is more comfortable. It is much easier and significantly more familiar to wage war than to wage peace.

Inasmuch as choosing peace on an international scale would fundamentally change the world, choosing peace on a personal level will fundamentally change your experience of the world. Like I said, the macrocosm and the microcosm are the same thing. While you can't do much to directly impact the international situation, you can do something about your own. If enough people choose to live a life of peace and possibility on a personal level, critical mass alone will change the international level.

I also very clearly understand that seeking the possibility of worldwide peace and prosperity is quite a dream. Some would say it is an unrealistic dream. But like George Bernard Shaw said:

"You see things; and you say, "Why?" But I dream things that never were; and I say, "Why not?"

Just for the record, I'd like to give you a small list of some other things that were merely unrealistic dreams for a very long time.

Man walking on the Moon.

Running a sub four minute mile.

Climbing Mount Everest.

Photographing the Titanic at the bottom of the sea.

The Boston Red Sox winning the World Series.

I sincerely believe we lost the best opportunity we have ever known to begin to create an atmosphere of world peace in the aftermath of 9/11. But the good news is that more opportunities will show themselves. I am reminded of a woman I heard on a radio talk show one day. She had written a book bemoaning the lack of available men with whom she could form a long-term relationship. It seemed that all the men she attracted to herself were emotionally unavailable, and she was having a very difficult time indeed. What she doesn't understand is that the world will continue to give her the same opportunity until she finally learns that the problem she is experiencing, and about which she had so thoughtfully written, has absolutely nothing to do with the men she is meeting. She will continue to get the opportunity to learn the lesson until she actually learns that it is she who has been unavailable - to herself and to the men in her life.

God has constructed our mortal existence as a magnificent laboratory in which our job is to learn the lessons we are given to learn. If we choose to respond to the same lessons in the same manner we have always responded, then we will most assuredly reap the same results. And the lesson will undoubtedly be provided to us again. The day we decide to learn the lesson and change the response is the day that the lesson will no longer come back to us. We will, of course, be given entirely new opportunities for learning and growth for which we will have the previously learned lessons from which to draw. It is like learning basic algebra and geometry before tackling the intricacies of trigonometry.

So, the same old lessons will be presented to us until we summon the courage and conviction necessary to look at the problem from a different perspective. Actually, we don't have to completely learn the lessons presented for significant per-

Chapter Five - Peace Is The Way

sonal growth to occur. God has wired this thing so well in our favor that all we have to do is become willing to learn and change. All we need to do is be willing, and God will take it from there. God is so loving and endlessly merciful that He has designed the game to work for us even if we are simply willing to look for another way. Remember, willingness to do creates the ability to do.

Not long after 9/11 I found myself once again in the office of my physical therapist. I was recovering from having knee surgery and was undergoing treatment that would help me to recover and begin training for triathlons again. On this particular day there was much discussion around the appropriate response to the events of 9/11 and the impending invasion of Iraq. Everyone in the room definitely came down foursquare on the side of violence, retaliation, and revenge. Everyone except me.

Now, I could very well have taken the easier, softer way and kept my mouth shut. I could have remained silent and allowed everyone present to continue on in their bliss of small thinking. But the events of 9/11 have irrevocably changed me and changed my life so that silence in the face of misunderstanding and error is no longer an option for me. I feel as though I have an obligation to help those whose paths I cross by at least offering an alternative to their lifelong habit of default thinking and unquestioned allegiance to maintaining some semblance of the status quo.

There really is no safety in allowing our thinking to go unchallenged because such a position first creates - then inevitably shrinks - the boundaries we use to define ourselves to ourselves.

It is in challenging our thinking, obliterating the status quo, and remembering that insanity is doing the same thing over and over again but expecting different results, that we begin to change the world.

As the conversation at my physical therapist's office developed, it became clear that everyone at first thought I was some sort of nut case, someone to be politely tolerated while conveying to me in no uncertain terms that my opinion was simply not welcome. Nobody wants to hear about the value and power of the peaceful response when they want to nuke an entire population. How could I ever come down on the side of peace in the face of such a heinous crime as 9/11? How did I ever get my wiring so screwed up in the first place? What was wrong with me?

Well, I made my case for ending the cycle of violence and retaliation that would only guarantee more of the same. Then I decided to let the chips fall where they may.

Finally, one of the women in the room asked me how I could ever expect to bring peace to the world. How is it possible, she asked me, to change the world? How could anyone ever expect to do such a thing? Underlying her question was the belief that it was much easier to go along and hope that everything would work itself out than to feel the enormous frustration of trying to do the impossible and actually change the world. Changing the world is just too big a task.

I replied that the world can be changed one person at a time, one day at a time, one thought at a time.

After a few minutes of relative silence in the room and while she was preparing to leave, she walked over to where I was having my treatment and told me that I had given her much to think about. She thanked me and told me that I may very well have changed her life. It doesn't get much better than that.

Living a life of peace in a peaceful world requires making a decision on a daily basis to accept nothing less than peace for yourself. This can be accomplished one situation at a time by asking yourself which response to this particular situation will bring you peace. The question always has an answer, and it is an answer that will never disappoint you, never leave you feeling less than, and never give you a feeling of helplessness, guilt, or remorse. And it is an answer that will never cause harm to another individual.

Once you make a decision to accept nothing less than peace in your life and you make a real commitment to carry out that decision, no matter what, your world will change. You will eventually find yourself in a similar place to that which I found myself on the morning of 9/11/2001. It was a morning when the vast majority of the people in America saw only the need for retaliation, revenge, and a continuation of the cycle of violence. It was a morning when I saw only the unfailing promise of peace, opportunity, prosperity and possibility. It was a morning when I finally realized that I had embraced the peaceful response as a way of life and saw only an incredible opportunity to change the world for the better.

You will turn around and one day be amazed to find that your capacity for vengeful, hateful, rage-filled and violent thought has virtually disappeared. Fear of the future will become a thing of the past. And you will then know peace. By choosing peace every day you will know the unlimited power that living a life of peace promises.

I wish you well on your journey.

THE SERENITY PRAYER

God grant me the serenity
to accept the things I cannot change;
courage to change the things I can;
and wisdom to know the difference.

Living one day at a time;
Enjoying one moment at a time;
Accepting hardships as the pathway to peace;
Taking, as He did, this sinful world
as it is, not as I would have it;
Trusting that He will make all things right
if I surrender to His Will;
That I may be reasonably happy in this life
and supremely happy with Him
Forever in the next.

Amen.

PRAYER OF SAINT FRANCIS

Lord, make me an instrument of your peace.
Where there is hatred, let me sow love;
where there is injury, pardon;
where there is doubt, faith;
where there is despair, hope;
where there is darkness, light;
and where there is sadness, joy.

O Divine Master, grant that I may not so much seek
to be consoled as to console;
to be understood as to understand;
to be loved as to love.
For it is in giving that we receive;
it is in pardoning that we are pardoned;
and it is in dying that we are born to eternal life.

Amen.